Well-Founded Fear

The Explorations in Feminism Collective

Kythe Beaumont
Jane Cholmeley
Claire Duchen
Renate Duelli-Klein
Catherine Itzin
Diana Leonard
Caroline Waller

Well-Founded Fear

A community study of violence to women

Jalna Hanmer and
Sheila Saunders

Hutchinson

in association with
The Explorations in Feminism Collective

affiliated to the
Women's Research and Resources Centre

London Melbourne Sydney Auckland Johannesburg

Hutchinson & Co. (Publishers) Ltd

An imprint of the Hutchinson Publishing Group

17–21 Conway Street, London W1P 6JD

Hutchinson Publishing Group (Australia) Pty Ltd
PO Box 496, 16–22 Church Street, Hawthorne, Melbourne
Victoria 3122

Hutchinson Group (NZ) Ltd
32–34 View Road, PO Box 40–086, Glenfield, Auckland 10

Hutchinson Group (SA) (Pty) Ltd
PO Box 337, Bergvlei 2012, South Africa

First published 1984

Photoset in Plantin Roman by
Kelly Typesetting Limited, Bradford-on-Avon, Wiltshire

Printed and bound in Great Britain by
Anchor Brendon Ltd, Tiptree, Essex

British Library Cataloguing in Publication Data
Hanmer, Jalna
  Well-founded fear.
  1. Women—England—Leeds—Crimes against
  2. Violence—England
  I. Title   II. Saunders Sheila
  364.1′5553   HV6250.4.W65
ISBN 0 09 155041 6

We dedicate this book to women in prisons everywhere who are locked up for murdering violent men

Contents

Figures and tables

Figures

Tables

Acknowledgements

We wish to thank all the women who contributed to this study. With special thanks to Jenny Wardleworth, Sandra McNeill, Marianne Hester, Lesley Kay and Al Garthwaite who, along with us, interviewed women in the neighbourhood; Diane Hudson and Annie Smith who produced the cartoons and other visuals used in this book; Petra Copland for the cartoon reproduced on p. 46; Hector Breeze for the cartoon reproduced on p. 23; and Ruth Bundy whose practical and personal support we particularly valued. We also wish to thank the South Headingley Community Association for their help and advice; the Bradford Law Centre and Marguerite Russell for information on criminal offences; and the Ella Lyman Cabot Trust (USA) for their initial financial support.

1. Researching our lives

The main aim of this book is to encourage women's groups to undertake their own research into violence to women. We will show that good research can be done by non-academics and that it is not always necessary to rely on either educational institutions or the state for funding or resources. This discussion will be based on our experiences of a community study of violence to women in Leeds in 1981.

Violence to women is an intensely political area in which to research. We think it is necessary to write this book because the research that is and has been commissioned, by and large, either misrepresents the true situation (for example, the British Crime Survey to be discussed later, see below, pp. 102–3), or is for double-checking publically available information from agencies that serve women (for example, the use of funds by the Department of Health and Social Security to study violence in marriage; see below, pp. 86–100; and Jalna Hanmer and Diana Leonard, forthcoming).

There are no trusts that have a special interest in funding research on women. The government agency with particular responsibility for women is the Equal Opportunities Commission, but they are reluctant to spend their limited funds on research into violence to women (see below, p. 106). Money is not being made available to study the extent of the problem, how the work of effective groups can be extended, and how bad state services can be improved. We conclude that the interests of existing power-holders, largely men, are being served by knowing as little as possible about violence to women. With this book we hope to extend our knowledge as women and challenge male control. We begin by describing the research on which the book is based. We discuss our experiences in finding ways of gaining information and the issues and

---

Full references quoted in text are contained in the Selected further reading beginning on p. 109.

problems that we encountered. We go on to describe how women see violence to themselves and to other women. We feel it is essential to throw some light on the mystery of why women expect and seek protection from men, the very group that abuses us. The next section describes the ways in which the state steps in when men attack women. The aim is to increase our understanding of how male violence to women is socially constructed to perpetuate itself. Finally, we show that the perpetuation of male violence to women is a circular system rooted in the division between the private and public spheres of life for women. We show the importance of the division to the process by which women are driven into greater dependence on men both individually and collectively, and how this serves to make women more vulnerable to attack. We then discuss how we think feminist groups can undertake further research on violence to women. We have also reproduced the questions used in our study for your information along with a list of others working on violence, research projects yet to be completed and suggestions for research from Women's Aid Federation England. We hope this will give you even more ideas about what you can find out about violence to women.

2. Them and us: conventional research methods versus feminist research

Information about male violence can be produced in more than one way by feminists, either through projects to help survivors of violence or through systematic information seeking. We suggest that both are necessary and both lead to further action, but at this point we need to know more about the actual extent of violence to women. It is likely to be far greater than we imagine, even today after a decade of public exposure. The work of Women's Aid and Rape Crisis centres, set up specifically to help women who are under attack from particular men, have produced estimates of unreported crime which suggest that only a very small proportion is reported to or discovered by the police. (London Rape Crisis Reports 1977, 1978 and 1982; and Women's Aid Federation England 1981).

Unreported crime is always referred to as the 'dark figure', and it was this that we set out to uncover. We also wanted to bring together the various forms of violence to women, so that we could see the patterns. Previous studies had focused on either public or private forms of violence and little has been done to explore their relationship with each other (Hanmer 1978).

We decided to undertake the study within a small local area for several reasons. We needed to try an approach that suited our limited funds. There was only enough money to meet interviewers' expenses and a few other costs such as a telephone, stationery, postage, etc. We wanted to ensure that the selection of women would not in and of itself define the type of violence and its amount (or incidence). Thus referrals from Women's Aid or Rape Crisis or any other supporting bodies that help survivors of violence were ruled out because labelling has already occurred. We also felt that community-based interviewing would help us explore ways that other groups of women, without funding, could undertake similar projects and enable us to carry on unfunded if necessary.

In the true tradition of community work we gathered information and then proceeded to feed it back into the community of women from which it came. We hoped that the community focus would help to develop new forms of self-help and mutual aid among women with community-wide initiatives aimed at self-protection and campaigns directed at the police and relevant sectors of local government, such as councillors, social workers, etc. The sharing of knowledge on the information gathering process and the results of the study formed the basis of the way in which these aims were to be achieved.

A community study, no matter how limited, was a new way of gaining information on violence to women. We set up the project knowing that previous studies have concluded that the most difficult area in which to gain information is on violence between people, as opposed to property offences. An American study, *Issues in the Measurement of Victimisation*, provides a comprehensive review of the issues involved (Skogan 1981). It is generally agreed that there is severe undercounting of assaults, which means that fewer assaults are reported to interviewers than actually take place. Frequent assaults on the same person by the same aggressor (domestic violence is the obvious example) are even less likely to be reported to researchers. The work of Sparks, Genn and Dodds (1977), the only British study to be completed when we began our interviewing, concluded that 'victims' of violence were more likely to refuse to be interviewed if they are women.

As we did not know how willing women would be to talk about their experiences of violence, we selected a city where we thought our chances of finding women who were prepared to do so would be good. The last so-called 'Ripper' murder seemed to raise consciousness of violence to women in the Leeds–Bradford area in a way that had not occurred with the previous murders. We felt that the murder of the Leeds University student, Jacqueline Hill, at 9 p.m. in December 1980 near a busy shopping precinct and main road had sensitized women to violence from men by disturbing all our understandings about what constitutes safe behaviour.

We chose a nearby inner city area in Leeds, but not the most deprived. We decided to interview every woman on seven adjacent streets rather than attempt some other form of sampling. The community aims of the study together with the need for careful piloting made this the best use of our limited resources. The streets had a mixed population of white single and married people, with and without children, living in multi-occupied as well as single-family houses. We felt it was important to focus on the problem of the dominant cultural group in order to avoid our results being used in a racist way. The survey area included a total of 171 houses and resulted in 129 completed questionnaires. Interviews took place between March and July 1981, after Peter Sutcliffe, the so-called 'Ripper', had been arrested and during his trial.

Because we were researching into violence we decided we would not ask for information that could identify the woman. We thought this might reduce our chances of gaining sensitive detail. We therefore asked interviewers to estimate the age of the woman and to write down any volunteered information on occupation, education, life-style, etc. At the end of the interview we asked if the woman lived alone or with others, including children, and noted whether or not she lived in multi-occupied or shared housing.

Women of all age groups lived within the chosen streets. Although the sample was skewed towards the younger, highly educated and childless woman, 10 per cent of those interviewed were elderly women, many of whom were living alone. But only one woman lived in a house on her own with children. Women were without paid employment, in jobs considered to be both middle and working class or were students at the nearby university or polytechnic. While we interviewed women from a range of backgrounds, women with children living with men or on their own were particularly under-represented. Table 1 shows that most women were living in shared or multi-occupied housing and that most were living with another adult rather than children or alone.

While we believed that women in the area were more aware of violence from men, we prepared the ground carefully with the community aspect of the project very much in mind. We visited the organizations in the area and in Leeds generally that we knew were working either in the neighbourhood or on violence to women. Women

Table 1 *Living arrangements of interviewed women*

	Living with adult	Living with children	Living alone	Shared or multi-occupied housing
Yes	84	19	13	116
No	45	110	116	13

councillors, lawyers, social workers and probation workers were also consulted about the project and we asked for their advice. A woman gave us the use of a room and telephone in her home so that we had an office and postal address. We leafletted the houses where we intended to interview women, leaving a telephone number where we could be contacted. We went on local radio and gave details of the project and were written about in the local press. We did not know how much information, if any, would be acquired in this way and we wanted to explore the possibilities. We also saw this as another way of introducing the idea of the survey into the neighbourhood.

The radio show resulted in a telephone call from a woman who was being beaten at the time of the broadcast. She kept repeating the number to herself until she was able to telephone. We immediately arranged for her to go to a Women's Aid refuge. Another woman in the area gave us a series of interviews about her married life, the physical and mental violence inflicted by her husband, and the way in which she had slowly restricted his capacity to abuse her while continuing to live with him. She also introduced us to another woman. With a larger area in mind and a different focus we might have been able to build up a network of interviews with abused and dissatisfied women who remain in their marriages. However, we decided to concentrate our meagre resources on interviewing in the seven streets.

The first interviewing problem we found proved to be our major difficulty: when to find women at home. Given that many women were single and childless, the difficulty of finding women at home was greater than it would have been in an area of families with young children. We began by calling between 11 a.m. and 4 p.m. on the assumption that we would be more likely to find women on their own, but with the exception of the elderly few were at home. Early evening proved to be the best time for contacting working women and students as many were out later in the evening. Several households consisted of nurses on shift work and we had great difficulty in establishing a suitable time to call. By and large interviewing had to take place between 5 and 7 p.m. We made repeated calls, never less than three, varying the time of day, but we still did not succeed in contacting every woman in the area. We did not call after dark even though it might have been the only time to contact some women. This was both to protect our interviewers and to avoid alarming the women themselves.

We met very few refusals. Those we had came from three sources.

Elderly women might not even open the door, but twitch the curtains so we could see that someone was at home. The same response occurred in almost all the few Asian households. There were sometimes problems of conflicting demands on a woman's time if women were living with men who were at home and our call coincided with preparing the evening meal. A few women refused on the grounds that they were not interested. Other women gave us interesting information while refusing to be interviewed. For example, Sandra McNeill was told by one elderly woman that she could not help because she never went out. Anyway, 'Coronation Street' was about to come on television. Sandra asked her if she would go out if it were safe.

Of course if it was safe I would go out. I'm 75. So I don't go out at all after dark. In winter, as soon as it's dark I stay in. You are not safe even in your own homes. What else can we do?

I blame the TV and those awful films and all the things they produce [porn]. They show no films with kindness towards people [in them]. It's all violence to animals and people. I think it would make things safer if they showed other films. When did you last see a film in which kids were being kind to old people? They tell you you must just accept change. But how are kids to learn? They should show films with kindness instead of these films and plays. It's just wrong.

They say, 'Oh but you don't need to watch'. But what else is there but the TV for old people? You can't go out on the streets. I'd like to go and see a friend. It's not far to go. You'd like to go but you can't go.

This sex business. It's all in the mind. Sex is nothing new. I mean how else would we all be here? But as for these films! Now I'm all for enlightenment. I believe in the enlightenment of the young, they should know something about sex. We were very ignorant when I was 17–18. I didn't know any facts of life. But this sort of thing . . . things being done to maim people! And the things you read in the paper about the elderly being attacked, elderly women. You don't feel safe at home. I still work you know, one evening a week, a friend escorts me in winter. I'd go out more – my friend lives just over the road but you don't feel you can safely. ['Coronation Street' music begins] You'll have to go now . . . this is all the recreation we have.

Another elderly woman said: 'This is not a violent neighbourhood. You should go with your questionnaire to Chapeltown [it is just after the riots] or to one of the estates. This is a nice neighbourhood.'

Sandra asked her if she felt safe if she did go out alone.

No of course not, not after dark no-one does round here. Everyone keeps the door locked. [The door was on the chain – during the day.] I only opened the door as I thought it was the gas man. Of course I don't go out at night. I just go out Thursdays for my pension that's all. I don't know anything, about violence. Go and ask in Chapeltown.

In the five streets where information on refusals was systematically gathered the total refusal rate from all these sources was 16 per cent.

Having discovered that the first hurdle, obtaining an interview, was not too difficult, we then had to establish effective contact. We wanted to interview women on their own but given the nature of women's lives this was not always possible. As a number of calls had to be made in the early evening, on occasion men stayed in the room answering questions for their wives or girlfriends. Neither they nor the interviewer were always able to challenge this situation successfully. This, however, was not as great a problem as we had feared in advance.

A major problem was interviewing women who were suffering regular violence, most probably from the men with whom they were living. However, as we have learned from the experiences of Women's Aid even when a woman no longer lives with a man he will often return to terrorize her. The academic language for this type of regular violence is 'series violence', and we experienced the same problems with series violence as the US national crime surveys. Skogan comments that 'victimizations' are seen by researchers as distinct incidents with a beginning and an end and limited in space and time. As a result he says that the survey form of information gathering does not accurately measure continuous processes that are not so clearly defined and that resemble enduring conditions rather than particular events.

We found that when series violence was in the past the problem became one of disentangling the incidents and limiting responses to the chosen time period of one year. If the violence was still going on the woman could be upset, making it difficult to find out what was really happening. On occasion the questions could not be asked in numerical order and they could seem trivial in the atmosphere. The interviewer was sometimes afraid of 'blowing the woman's cover', of further upsetting her, or of starting something the interviewer felt she might be unable to cope with. This rarely happened, but a process of minimizing or underplaying the situation was an aspect of many interviews.

Partly to overcome this problem and to offer some support we organized a regular group meeting for those women who seemed to be experiencing either current long-term difficulties or acute violent experiences that remained unresolved, perhaps because unshared. While there was some interest and several women came together for short periods of time, this did not really work. We always left leaflets from Women's Aid and Rape Crisis when women did not know about these services or how to contact them. For ethical and for practical reasons to do with the women's safety, we did not call again on women whose interviews had caused us deep concern.

Some women may be more willing to talk to a complete stranger. They may want to talk about violence used against them as a way of dealing with the experience and the hurt. A woman may feel that someone is actually interested in her feelings and her fears. To ask questions about the incident(s) is to validate her experience. It is a public recognition of the violence used against her. But asking too many questions could cause alarm by raising the experience to a level that produces an unwanted crisis. It would be wrong to get into a situation where the interviewer is pushing for more details. The interviewer should allow women to dictate the terms of the interview, and give them space within which to maneouvre. Women interviewing women is a two-way process. Jenny Wardleworth illustrates these points by her comments on one particularly difficult interview.

Straight away this woman was cautious, suspicious and sceptical. Her movements were nervous, erratic and she was generally edgy. In this atmosphere of distrust and nervousness I found it difficult to ask her questions. I have not completed the questionnaire properly because of this. [See the questionnaire, pp. 80–5.]

Question 1   She was very indignant about having to suffer being scared and restricted. 'It is not always possible to be accompanied by someone when going out', etc.

Question 2   When I asked her Question 2 she said, 'No, but what about myself? Does that count?' As she spoke she sounded bitter and slightly incoherent. I said I would come to that in a moment.

Question 3   Very quickly I turned to Question 3 and got it over with so that I could ask her what she meant.

Question 4   I asked Question 4 and she began to relate the tale of being grabbed by her hair. This by the guy she lives with I think. It was while they were coming home, probably, as she said it happened in a street near here. It happened quite recently. I *feel* sure it is *not an isolated incident* from her manner and from subsequent talking. When I asked her about getting help, she told me in a trapped sounding voice that she wasn't in any position to. I gathered it was her boyfriend who stays now and then. After this occasion he went away to his own place. She says she did not report it because she is giving him a second chance. If he did it again that would be it. During this period she was tidying up.

She told me that she had been badly beaten and battered by her husband, over a year ago. She seemed bitter that I was asking about this past year, so I wrapped up the incident with her boyfriend and got on to what she wanted. I then began to ask her questions about the previous beatings from her husband. By this time she sat down and began drinking from a bottle of cider and smoking continuously. She said she did not want to talk much about the previous battering from her husband because she had just found out he had died. This was a shock to her: 'I am a widow. I have just found out I am a widow.'

Questions 5 and 6 I asked her Questions 5 and 6. She hesitated and eventually said, she didn't think so. (!) So . . . I began to talk about the whole general situation of domestic violence so I could get more information and also in answer to her questions. Some of her questions were difficult for me to answer owing to my lack of experience and many were rhetorical. For example, 'If a woman goes to an agency somewhere for help how can she prevent the facts from involving the perpetuator who may then get annoyed and repeat the beatings? . . . When a woman is living with a violent man, she is too scared to ask for help. . . . Sometimes living with a violent man is an alternative to living alone. . . . To save a relationship you may put up with violence, hoping it is worth it.'

I think she may be seeing a bloke who is violent. She seemed tense once and stared at the door, at a noise outside. She could have done with Women's Aid before. Her past has made her bitter and impatient. For now I suggested that she joined the support group we were forming to offer continuing help to women in her situation. She replied, 'Not yet, I can't yet.' I gave her the Rape Crisis Centre leaflet and Women's Aid leaflets. I urged her to make use of these as tactfully and diplomatically as I could as she is not admitting to being beaten now. I told her someone else would be willing to come around and talk to her, or offer her advice, etc. after I had asked if she wanted someone more knowledgeable to come and see her.

Question 7 In answer to Question 7 she said, 'People damage things through being drunk, etc. . . . There is not much you can do when someone comes home from drinking all night and accuses you of things.' She was talking about her husband.

This interview was very difficult and I could not follow the questionnaire properly. The questions seemed trivial in the atmosphere. I was afraid of 'blowing her cover', upsetting her, or starting something I could not cope with. She is in her 30s. An office worker. She was insistent at the outset that the questionnaire be confidential. I think she may contact us, but I am not sure. She then showed me to another bedsit upstairs.

On reflection I think she was beaten in the past. She may be being harassed now in her relationship, but won't admit it. However, past experience tells, her whole manner and her drinking and smoking spoke volumes!!

(*Authors' note*:   an incident sheet was made out on the hair grabbing which involved her being knocked against a wall where her lip was cut. The incidents with the husband were outside our time limit and therefore not counted in our statistics.)

While interviewing, we came across women who had moved into the area to escape matrimonial violence, but by accident rather than design. Without doubt we interviewed others who were not there six months later for the same reasons. As Wesley Skogan notes, 'It is prosecutor's lore that the first response of many victims of crime is to arrange an unlisted telephone number or move to a new address' (1981, p. 14). In the US national crime surveys people who have recently moved report a higher rate of violence against them and a substantial proportion of those experiencing series violence move to another address before the next six monthly interview. In the UK this pattern is well known to those who help women who have been assaulted in their own homes, whether by strangers or known others. While we asked how long women had been in the neighbourhood, we should have followed this up by asking why they had moved.

We have no way of knowing how many violent encounters the women we interviewed experienced in the last year, but it is reasonable to assume that non-response through forgetting was an issue for several reasons. The questionnaire left the definition of violent events to women and what one woman might regard as a frightening experience another would not. As previous research would lead us to expect, the women interviewed recalled more incidents involving themselves than others. We asked for information over the past year. The US national crime surveys inquire about the last six months, and even for this period the non-response error is said to be considerable. While the results of surveys vary, from the conclusion that forgetting becomes a major

'Mr Windersley is a sociologist and Mr Mulcett here is his interpreter.'

problem after three months to only a slight decline over a ten month period, non-response is said to be much more of a problem for researchers than inaccurate answers, or mis-reponse.

While we cannot prove that inaccuracy, or mis-reponse, was more important than forgetting, or non-response, we believe this to be true. We encountered three types of mis-reponse. The first, well known in the literature on research methods, was confusion about time when recalling incidents. Events were brought forward in time, known as telescoping in research jargon. Both forgetting and forward telescoping combine to produce apparently decreasing rates of incidents over the length of the chosen period of time. To control telescoping material into and within the reference period, answers should be checked by reference to dates that are meaningful to the woman being interviewed, such as when she took her summer holiday, important family events or moving house. These questions are asked first, and then it is possible to say, for example, 'and this took place after your holiday?' It is possible to control telescoping by interviewing the same woman more than once and to control forgetting by limiting the period of time, neither of which we were able to do.

To estimate violence to women more accurately the general advice is either a small sample and a longer time period or a larger sample and a shorter time period. We needed enough information to be able to speak of violence in relation to the neighbourhood as well as to individual women, and the choice of a time period of one year was the usual compromise. It also coincided with the first murder of a university student by Peter Sutcliffe, Barbara Leach in Bradford, and a change in reporting by newspapers and television from the stress on prostitutes to the recognition that any woman could be a victim. The chosen area for interviewing had a high proportion of Leeds University students.

In many interviews women deliberately did not tell us about violent incidents that had happened to them. This was the second type of mis-response we encountered. Incidents are more likely to be reported when the aggressor is a stranger and less likely when he is known. The least reporting occurs when the aggressor and person harmed are related to each other. A US and a Canadian survey had surprisingly similar results. Stranger violence recall was 76 per cent and 71 per cent respectively, known parties 56 per cent in both surveys, and related parties 22 per cent and 20 per cent (Turner 1972; Catlin and Murray 1979). We know this happened because women were more likely to report violence within the neighbourhood as being between those known to each other or living together than they were for violence directed at themselves. For example, a woman might tell us that her upstairs neighbour had serious problems with her husband, but once upstairs no mention would be made of domestic troubles. Across twenty-six US cities 70 per cent of all interpersonal violence was attributed to strangers (Skogan 1981, p. 30). Evidence from other sources such as police data, however, indicates that a much higher proportion takes place between people known to each other. In Britain this is confirmed by the analysis of offences involving violence dealt with by the police in Edinburgh and Glasgow (Dobash and Dobash 1980). Also the information on relationship and murder provided by the Home Office annually shows that women are more likely to be murdered by known others (Criminal Statistics England and Wales).

There are many ways of interpreting why women suppress information concerning violence to them. Women may not want to remember a painful situation, or may not want a story spread further, or the event may be seen as non-criminal. We believe that women are even more likely to take the responsibility for attacks from men known or related to them than they are for stranger violence, although this factor is never entirely eliminated (see below, pp. 52–3). We do not think that so-called victim precipitation, that is, negligence, foolish or culpable actions on the part of women determines the willingness of women to respond, but rather the assumptions that women make about personal responsibility. Victim blaming, widespread in the media, shows that our culture holds women responsible for the violent behaviour of men, and this increases with the closeness of the relationship. It is not surprising that women as well as men comply with, or embrace, this dominant cultural value given the near unanimity of opinion.

We do not think women invent incidents or deliberately lie, fabri-cating stories of violent assault. The issue of mis-response is more subtle. The third type of mis-response that affected our results was the reconstruction of events, or how an incident is remembered after it has happened. We found that the women interviewed tended to minimize the importance of violent events, which we felt was a way of handling fear, frustration and anger. It was often impossible to fill in the incident form that accompanied the questionnaire. To do so would be to magnify the incident (this is discussed above, pp. 20–2) and give it an importance that the woman did not want, or so the interviewer felt. Often incident sheets would be filled in on some violent events but not others. A 'by the way', a casual throwaway remark would reveal a violent encounter while signalling that a request for more details would be unacceptable. Minimalizing marginalizes experience, which may be necessary for a woman to maintain her sense of security within a personal relationship and to conform with a commonly held view that there is something wrong with a woman if a man starts to hit her.

It also puts into context the discussion on how interviewers affect the interview and why some of those interviewed produce more information than others. Some interviewers have been found to be better at gaining reports of series violence than others, but the reasons for this are complex. To use our study as the example, we had six women inter-viewers and the bulk of the interviews were undertaken by three women. We regarded women interviewers as essential to help women take their experiences seriously and thus reduce minimalizing for two reasons. The power imbalance automatically built into a social situation where one person interviews another is partly reduced if both parties are women. On a more conscious level, we felt that women would be less likely to minimize the importance of incidents if talking to another woman. If interviewers had been men the superior status of men, together with the need to defer to their feelings when discussing the subject of male violence, would have made it very difficult to acquire any information.

All the women interviewers were white feminists, between the ages of 30 and 50, and all had been through higher education. We looked for women who knew that violence to women is a reality and who were knowledgeable about women's organizations offering support. We also thought it essential that all of us were motivated to work on the project because of a desire to know in a more systematic way about women's experiences of violence. We needed interviewers who would behave in a sensitive manner, and convey a feeling of warmth and unflappability; people in whom it was possible to confide without damage being done to them. (For a clear and feminist discussion of the issues involved in interviewing women and women interviewers see Ann Oakley's article, 1981.)

Previous research in the US indicates that better educated people living in the suburbs experience more crime than poorer inner city people. These results are considered to be inaccurate, reflecting the education and class of those interviewed rather than genuine differences in the experience of crime. We do not know how these factors affect women's responses. While many of the women we interviewed were in, or had experienced higher education, many had not and still gave us interviews and information. We could not detect any social factor either encouraging or discouraging reporting once an interview was granted.

A general issue in interviewing is a tendency for those interviewed to agree, or say the things that they think are expected of them, or to please the interviewer by producing some relevant information. The problem may be intensified when interviewing women, because a passive submission epitomizes femininity. While the socially acceptable reply would be no experience of violence, the need to give a helpful answer once in an interview situation may become more prominent. Hilary Graham, after interviewing women about family planning, suggests that moving beyond the acceptable response is achieved by gaining the answer to the question, pausing, and then writing down what the woman really thinks as she will often give additional material once the culturally approved answer is given. Something like this occurred in some of our interviews in that an incident would be mentioned towards the end of an interview during a question about other aspects of violence to women. This may reflect the fact that women find it difficult to speak about themselves. We introduced the subject of violence by inquiring whether the woman had witnessed or overheard violence to others. We thought this would give the woman an opportunity to talk about herself in the third person if she wished to do so, as well as lead on to a discussion of experienced violence.

As discussed earlier, women were much more likely to report violence between those known to each other than between strangers when talking about what they had witnessed or overheard in the neighbourhood; but when discussing their own experiences violence from strangers played a larger role. While these two types of questions served as a useful cross-check, we are left with incomplete information on violence from known men. The introduction to our questionnaire referred to the so-called 'Ripper' murders and the first questions asked about feelings and changes in behaviour. These early questions may have implied to the women being interviewed that we were particularly interested in, or defining, violence as public stranger attacks.

We might have increased the overall amount of information if we had asked about all types of violence and then produced the incident sheets asking for detail about each violent attack. Research shows that if those being interviewed have to work harder, or if they can easily learn how to reduce the workload, they will respond by restricting the amount of information given. One study showed an increase in reported incidents of two-and-a-half times by seeking details afterwards (Skogan 1981).

Our research shows a series of problems and issues. Some are ethical and some are to do with method. The material that we have gathered casts some light on processes that may further feminist research and theory. We do not claim to have measured the true incidence of violence experienced by the interviewed women, although we regard our results as showing important connections between individual women and the state, and between men and women. To improve the quality of the data and to better understand the issues surrounding methods, sociologists recommend research designs that double-check information and ways of gaining it. Two good methods are record checks and experimental research designs.

One strategy in double-checking information is to refer to another set of records that cover the same group to be researched, but this is not possible for research into violence to women in the locality. For example, in our study we monitored the local and some national press systematically for accounts of violence to women. We also acquired permission for limited access to some court records. But neither of these sources, nor police records had we had access, would be effective. The media by its selective attention and form of presentation serves to structure and restrict understanding of violence to women. The form this takes, of course, is important to compare alongside the actual experiences of women, but that serves another purpose. Given the low reporting rate, neither police files nor court records would provide an alternative source of information on violence. Crime surveys suggest that only 50 per cent of all serious crimes are reported to the police and even fewer so-called less serious crimes. In our study the reporting rate was much lower.

The other strategy, experimental design, would involve varying particular aspects of gaining information across different groups of women. These groups would need to be chosen so that every woman had an equal chance of being chosen, that is random selection. If two randomly chosen groups were approached for information in different ways, it would be possible to compare the effectiveness of these differences. However, this type of research would require proper funding and we cannot expect the state and the men who manage it in the interests of other men, to provide adequate research money to expose what we see as the male protection racket.

We suggest that women's groups need to undertake research into violence to women in the localities in which they live. We suggest that you devise a questionnaire which seems most suited to your needs and your area, bearing in mind the successes and failures of others, and go out and test it. If enough women's groups do this, we can begin to compare approaches, questions, interviewing skills and results across a number of small local projects. To replace record checks, at least in part, we suggest the continued presence of women's groups collecting information on violence to women in local areas using a variety of ways of gathering information over a period of time.

While some money always helps, and we had a grant of £1000, we think this work can be undertaken unfunded, especially if your group has access to office equipment and supplies free of charge. This is often possible to arrange as many groups of women know. If a little money is available from your local council, local trust, or wherever, we suggest spreading the funds through a larger group by paying interviewers, for typing, analysis of information etc., rather than using all the money to pay one person to be the researcher. The more women who gain experience in researching into the local area, the more women there will be to carry on the action after the results are known.

In Chapter 7 we will look at the issues we think will be important for you to think about in setting up your research. A copy of our questionnaire is included as well as suggestions for changes based on our experience.

3. Women's views on and experiences of violence

Defining violence is extremely difficult. Reaching any agreement on a definition is even more difficult. Individual and collective agreements about the use of violence in certain circumstances vary enormously when confronted with specific situations. Women have experienced these variable responses in their dealings with the police and others who provide services for victims of violence such as doctors, nurses, health visitors and social workers. They are observed in women actually involved in violent situations, and among their families, friends and the general public. Borkowski, Murch and Walker have looked into these variable responses in their research on marital violence (1983) as has Mary Maynard (forthcoming). In our study we did not want to predetermine the meaning of the term violence. We wanted women to define violence for themselves. We wanted to know about the experiences of women and the lines that they drew around their experiences. We therefore used a variety of words to trigger responses on aggressive episodes to encourage women to talk about these experiences. In the interviews we moved from threats, to violence, to sexual harassment.

It would be very simple if we were able to accept the legal definitions of violent crime as set out by the criminal law in Britain. However, even with this seemingly tidy solution there is no general agreement on the interpretation of the law, or the categories of behaviour to be labelled violent, or their seriousness, or whether actual situations are criminal offences. In research on victims (known by social scientists as victimology) there is no agreement on what a crime is or how it can be measured or analysed. For feminists the task is perhaps more clearly defined, as we understand and agree that the law and its enforcement is male (as well as class and racially) biased. It was with this knowledge in mind that we proceeded.

Most importantly, the type of aggression, the main organizing principle for the criminal justice system's categorization of crimes

'Women at bus stops are waiting for buses.
Get it?!

against the person, is not the major principle used by the women interviewed. Because the basis for defining behaviours as violent differs, the women interviewed classed as threatening, violent or sexually harassing situations that fell outside the criminal law as well as within it. For example, an attempted pick-up in the street (pp. 40–1) and in the home (p. 41). There were even some reports of situations where the criminal justice system would have prosecuted the woman as well as, or rather than, the man if they had known of the offence. For example, we were told of one incident where a man in a pub was verbally abusive, and the woman physically assaulted him by breaking a beer glass over his head. She viewed this as self-defence, but the criminal justice system would not.

The women we interviewed reported a wide range of behaviour which they perceived as threatening, violent or sexually harassing. Two-thirds of our sample reported one or more incidents that they had experienced or witnessed or overheard happening to other women during the past year, a total of 211 incidents. Table 2 summarizes the incidence and distribution of violent experiences.

Over half reported one or more experiences of violence to themselves in the past year. As we might expect there were fewer reports of violence to other women either witnessed or actually overheard. Because we were interested in personal experience, we did not seek information on violence women may have heard about from the media or friends (we discuss problems of inaccurate answers on pp. 23–5).

Table 3 shows the frequency of violent experiences. On average each woman experienced 1.6 incidents.

Table 2 *Incidence of violence to self and others*

	Violence experienced or witnessed			No violence experienced	
	Number of incidents	*Number of women*	%	*Number of women*	%
To others	70	47	36	82	64
To self	141	76	59	53	41
Total	211	84*	65	45*	35

* As some women reported both violence to themselves and others the total number of women is less than the sum of the column.

Table 3 *Distribution of responses of incidents*

	Number of incidents								Total women
	1	2	3	4	5	6	7	8	
Number of women reporting	29	23	12	12	3	2	2	1	84

We looked at violent events in two ways, as told to us in response to our questionnaire and according to the dominance of visual, verbal or physical elements in the encounter. Table 4 shows how women responded to our questions about experiences of threats, violence and sexual harassment.

Sexual harassment accounted for three-fifths of the incidents and two-fifths of all women interviewed reported this type of experience. Threats made up a quarter of the incidents and were experienced by a quarter of the women interviewed. Physical violence was least reported, just under one-sixth of all incidents and women interviewed.

The common strand running through these events is the inability of the woman to control the initiation of the behaviour and the subsequent interaction. While we did not attempt to measure how frightened or out of control of the situation the women were, or believed themselves to be, it seemed that *the greater the uncertainty about the outcome the more terrifying the encounter.* We regard this as our first major finding as it is the only way to make sense of the differences between the importance women place on certain behaviours as against that of the police and courts.

Table 4 *Threats, violence and sexual harassment experienced by self*

Type of violence	Number of incidents	%	Number of women	% of all women interviewed
Threats	36	25	31	24
Violence	21	15	21	16
Sexual harassment	84	60	58	45
Total	141		76*	59*

* As some women reported more than one incident in more than one category the total number of women is less than the sum of the column.

Table 5   *Visual, verbal and physical violence experienced by self*

Type of violence	Number of incidents	%	Number of women	% of all women interviewed
Visual	36	25	28	22
Verbal	70	50	53	41
Physical	35	25	29	22
Total	141		76*	59*

* As some women reported more than one incident in more than one category the total number of women is less than the sum of the column.

These differences are shown more clearly when behaviour described as violent is categorized as visual, verbal or physical. Table 5 shows that a quarter of incidents were visual and a quarter involved physical assault. The other half were verbal encounters. The numbers of women who had experiences of these were similarly divided. Visual violence, where no, or minimal words are exchanged, and no physical contact occurs can be among the most frightening of incidents. Genital exposure and being chased or followed were not uncommon visual encounters interpreted as violent. Exposure of the male genitals, or flashing, may promote fears of injury and death to a woman on her own in an isolated part of an open space or deserted street because of her uncertainty about what may happen next. It is only after the encounter that the label flashing or 'only flashing' is put upon the event. Murder, rape, being seriously beaten up and/or sexually assaulted, may be the feared outcome while the encounter is going on.

Women can be threatened visually while they are in their own homes and the aggressor is outside; it is not necessary that they both occupy public space. For example, 'A man came and stood on the wall in front of the window and masturbated. Because I live on my own, with no back door, it was very threatening. I was terrified.' The fear was that he would somehow get into her home. In another incident, a man simply sat in a parked car outside a house occupied by three women for several hours. The three women reporting this incident, in separate interviews, feared that he was staking out their home with intent to follow up this action with some type of attack upon them. These examples illustrate not only how uncertainty about outcomes may affect interpretation, but also the lack of a sharp division between the public and private domestic location for the same type of violence.

Uncertainty about the outcome is influenced by a number of factors, such as: the woman's previous experience; how she is feeling about herself and the world; what takes place between her and the assailant – especially behaviour on his part that intensifies fear about his intentions; and the context itself. Assaulted women have various criteria to assess whether or not a situation is violent. These are:

1   Whether or not others are present.
2   The time.
3   The place.
4   Prior knowledge of particular individuals or groups of men as violent.
5   Whether or not the woman knows her assailant(s).

We will look at each of these conditions in turn.

The presence of others

If we consider indecent exposure, flashers have different techniques, some of which seem to be more terrifying than others. Those who make sexually oriented remarks to women may increase fears of further sexual attack in a way that asking for directions, or the time, or not speaking, may not. The presence of others may turn a situation that would be frightening for a woman alone, into a joke. For example:

I was with three girlfriends walking across the Moor [a local park] at dusk. A man overtook us and stopped further on. When we reached him his trousers and knickers were around his knees. He asked for the time. Two of us noticed and tried to pull the other two on as they had stopped to look at their watches. They thought we were being rude and we did not discover until later that they did not have their contact lenses in. It was so absurd. We had a good laugh about it afterwards.

The presence of others, however, does not always make a situation less frightening. It may make a situation more threatening if a responsibility for others is involved. One woman reported feeling more vulnerable when one of the local vagrants verbally abused her when she had her

'Looks like our Jimmy
flashed at the wrong woman this time'.

young child with her. In these circumstances she tried to avoid him, walking quickly away, although she thought it should have been possible to talk to him and possibly would have done so if the child had not been present.

The time of day or night

The time of an encounter appeared to affect women's view of it as violent. In the neighbourhood there are two categories of men who regularly abuse women during the day. The first is the flashers and the second is the vagrants who sit near the children's playground. Flashers must have some light, or they will not be seen. As the open space often used by them is unlit, they flash here during the day or early evening. The vagrants use the same open space, where women have observed them urinating while drunk in front of children. They also approach women for money and sometimes verbally abuse them. As we might expect, the amount of fear expressed by women varied. They expressed outrage that these events take place during the daylight hours. The expectation is that violence in public places happens at night; violence during the day is unexpected and illegitimate, therefore more significant and memorable. Other women expressed a different, but possibly related point of view, that threatening events occurring during the day are somehow more safe. For example:

I have been approached and followed by vagrants. You get a lot around here and they ask for money. I don't carry much on me so it's often true that I have none. But I put a pace on then. It happens quite frequently. If it were the other end of the day after they have been drinking I just would not go near somebody like that, but it's usually in the mornings around 8 a.m.

The place

Table 6 shows where violence occurred. Almost half of the women reported that incidents took place in streets and open spaces. When other public locations are included more than half of the reported encounters took place in public. We do not think these statistics are reliable, however, and have some proof of this as Table 6 shows a higher proportion of incidents occurring at home to neighbours than to the women interviewed. Also, we know from other sources, such as

Table 6 Incidence and location of violence to self and other women in past year

Incident occurred to	Home	%	Work	%	Public places pubs etc.	%	Streets, open spaces	%	Not clear	%	Total
							Location of violence				
Self	30	21	15	1	16	11	67	48	13	9	141
Others											
neighbourhood	15	36	—	—	—	—	25	60	2	4	42
Leeds generally	6	21	—	—	6	21	11	39	5	19	28
Total	51	24	15	7	22	10	103	49	20	10	211

Women's Aid and Home Office statistics, that women are more likely to be assaulted by men known to them than by strangers.

Public places are the province of strangers, where assumptions of shared values about social behaviour often cannot be made. For example: 'I was in the road and a man said, "You need a fuck"'; or 'I was shouted at down the street "take your knickers off"'; or 'One evening recently a man yelled at me that I was a whore for walking around at that time of night on my own'; or 'One afternoon walking across campus a man said, "Excuse me". I stopped and he said, "Can I sleep with you?"'; or 'I go out a lot with women. If you go around arm in arm you get a lot of obscene suggestions such as "You fucking lesbians" or "Can I join you, you need a prick in there"'; or 'Last winter when I was out alone towards dusk men in cars driving past would say things like "are you looking for Jack tonight? Why don't you come with me instead"' (see below, pp. 107–8); or "Do you want a lift? . . . some company? . . . where do you live? . . . where are you going?" There was definitely a lot more of it during the "Ripper" scare.'

Public space also includes pubs, clubs, railway stations and other buildings. Women described verbal incidents some of which escalated into physical encounters. One example involved a known man:

I went to a pub with a woman friend. Her ex-husband drinks there. He asked her to leave. He was drunk and got vicious and abusive to her and me. He didn't actually hit her but it got very close. We stayed in the pub and sat it out.

But this woman has not returned to that pub. Women's sense of security in public places is profoundly shaped by our inability to secure an undisputed right to occupy that space. The curtailing of movement is a not infrequent response to violent and threatening encounters in public.

Prior knowledge of particular individuals or groups of men as violent

Uncertainty, and thus fear, about the outcome of encounters can be increased by knowledge, either personal or by reputation, of particular men or groups of men. Incidents of non-verbal and verbal encounters include threats from husbands or other men who have physically harmed women in the past. For example, one woman helped a neighbour leave home for a Women's Aid refuge. She was later telephoned by the husband who threatened to 'come around and get her'. Another woman reported that while she did not know who rang her doorbell late at night, she thought it was someone who had 'hassled' her before. Being alone in the house, she was too frightened to answer, but he carried on ringing for over an hour. A telephone call to a place of work employing a number of women, saying, 'I'm the Ripper and I will get one of you next' illustrates an increase in fear caused by the reputation of a particular killer. Another woman working in a community alternative bookshop that had been attacked previously, reported several instances of threatening telephone calls and verbal abuse from men visiting the shop, some of whom were known to be in the British Movement, a neo-fascist organization. The level of their anger, the knowledge that she symbolized something hateful to such men, and her awareness of the violent outcome of encounters in similar bookshops, increased her fear.

Whether or not the woman knew her attacker

If we look first at the encounters with strangers, there were a number of accounts of women being unable to avoid verbal approaches from men while in public places, particularly the street, in addition to the visual events of following, chasing and sexual exposure. These were described as indecent, sexually harassing, or threatening. Also, obscene and threatening phone calls from strangers reached into the home and the workplace. Many women were in occupations that served the public; working as barmaids in pubs or behind social security counters, where verbal abuse from customers and clients is seen, in practice, as part of the job. But only a proportion of women mentioned this kind of behaviour which suggests to us a high tolerance level of a very wide-spread kind of abuse. Verbal assaults from strangers were sometimes accompanied by physical touching, bumping into, grabbing, and there were also assaults that were primarily physical including sexual attacks.

Women's behaviour and sense of personal security is profoundly shaped by their inability to control interactions with strangers. One young woman described an incident that illustrates this point and the individual variation in the perception of events.

I was waiting outside. . . . Hotel for my boyfriend one afternoon. I was there a little over 5 minutes when a man of about 30 came and stood about five yards away. It seemed as if he too was waiting for someone but I remember feeling uncomfortable. I think this was mainly because I often tend to get embarrassed when I have to wait for someone else by myself. After a couple of minutes he came over and asked if I had the time. I told him and then he asked if I was waiting for someone. I said yes. Then he asked if I fancied going with him for a good time. I didn't answer and moved further away, hoping this would make it clear that I wanted him to go away. He followed me and offered to buy me a drink. I said no and walked away to a different spot. This time he went away.

While she saw this incident as sexually harassing, it is highly unlikely that the man did. The recognition of behaviour as unacceptable, if not violent, is mediated by one's views on proper male and female behaviour. In our society men are expected to take the leading role and women to acquiesce with faint protest. Male aggressive dominance and female passive submission are cultural ideals. In this example he tried and she demurred, with no outward verbal or physical threat being offered. She, however, saw the situation as an intrusion, over which she had little control, which was also the reality. She could not stop the approach being made, and could not terminate it at will. Her discomfort sprung from uncertainty about what the other person would do next and an inability to control the interaction between them.

Threatening and violent situations between people known to each other were also of more than one type with women reporting verbal and physical encounters including sexual attacks. An example of a less obvious experience was given by a young woman who lived in a bed-sitting room house with a shared kitchen. She shows the difficulty of defining behaviour as threatening or violent when people know each other.

A chap in the house made advances while my boyfriend was away for a while. He asked if I felt lonely at night. He read me a story that he thought liberated, but I thought pornographic. I felt threatened then. I told a girlfreind who suggested that I move in with her until my boyfriend came back. But I thought, I've a lock on my door and if you always shy away from what you are afraid of you will never grow accustomed to coping.

An onlooker might see this woman's behaviour as collusive, but it is easy to become involved in ways not intended or anticipated, given personal knowledge and shared understandings that often exist between people known to each other. This example also illustrates how easy it is to restrict encounters with the same man when you can exclude him from your living space. The following, unfortunately typical, example already exposed by the work undertaken by refuges for battered women, shows how difficult this can be when living with a violent man. A woman married for twenty-two years reports:

I stood it for my kids. He began hitting me when I was pregnant. He was arrogant, ignorant and violent. He fractured my nose, broke my ribs, nearly strangled me, smashed up the furniture.

In the past year, as well as being violent at home, he threatened her at her place of work which resulted in the involvement of her employers and the police. Over the years her attempts to gain help from public agencies, including the church, proved fruitless.

Home, the location of known others and assumptions of shared values about social behaviour is well illustrated by this woman. 'Everyday life is different. You argue for a little while. It doesn't mean he is going to murder you. It is different to what happens outside. Nothing wild. Just arguments.' This view is completely at odds with statistical fact, however, as he is more likely than a stranger to murder her. Assaults by known others may not feel as threatening as the same behaviour from a stranger. For example,

There have been several incidents with a man I've known a long time. He likes to see more of me than I do of him. He does get aggressive.

[Specific incidents?] Well on occasions when I'm in a pub with other people he'll come over . . . . Or he has dropped around to see me. We've been arguing over the past trying to talk about it. He gets very upset. Very angry. Usually ends up hitting me. He always apologises after and hates himself for doing it. He has got a lot of problems in many other ways.

No police ever, usually other friends are around and have helped out. I would have called the police . . . it wouldn't help him. I feel it's the result of the rest of his life. He needs help but not the police.

Not only may women take responsibility for the violent man, they may also minimize the importance of being attacked by someone they know. One woman reporting on an argument with her husband said, 'I was beaten up, but not very much. I didn't suffer much from this.' It is unlikely that she would have made the same response to violence from a stranger.

The relevance of knowing or not knowing the aggressor is a complex factor. We assume that strangers may not share our values about acceptable behaviour, while the opposite is true for known others. The result is that it may feel safer to be abused by someone we know than by someone we do not. Women find violence from strangers less acceptable than violence from known men. Although when women decide the men they live with are dangerous, violence seems inescapable and therefore very frightening. Certainly women were more likely to report violence from strangers than from men they knew.

Women were more likely to report on violence they witnessed or overheard in the neighbourhood between men and women known to each other than they were about violence to themselves from people they knew. Table 7 shows the relationship between women and their aggressors. Comparing the percentages, 18 per cent of all violence to the self was from a known man, while 69 per cent of all witnessed or overheard violence in the neighbourhood involved those known to each other. This provides a partial cross-check on the relative amount of violence from strangers and known others. These results expose massive survey error, but no greater than that of other surveys. For example, the relative percentages of violence from strangers and known others are similar to those obtained by the successive national crime surveys in the United States. As would be expected Table 7 shows that women were less certain of relationships when reporting on incidents witnessed or overheard in Leeds generally than in the neighbourhood itself.

While women used these factors to define violence and threatening situations, and to grade their importance, we were struck by the similarity between types of violence, including intensity, that occurred in public and in private domestic places. We were also struck by the frequency with which violent and threatening behaviour began in one location and then spilled over into another. Thus violence at work may not be directly related to the workplace. We have mentioned women's employment in the service sector and were told of harassment between workmates. Women in work traditionally defined as appropriate for males also have problems. It may be necessary to be taken for 'one of the lads' to survive with male workers. Harassment from strangers can also occur as this example illustrates. A young woman taking a course in landscape architecture explains, 'You walk around a lot with a sketch book, often in derelict areas. Men come along and talk to you. You get strange fellows following you about. I have had trouble getting rid of them.' This included being followed home. And finally, violence unrelated to the work environment may also occur there as several earlier examples show.

Table 7 *The relationship between women and their aggressors*

Incident occurred to	Known	%	Unknown	%	Do not know	%	Total
Self	25	18	110	78	6	4	141
Others							
neighbourhood	29	69	2	5	11	26	42
Leeds generally	9	32	5	18	14	50	28
Total	63	30	117	55	31	15	211

Violence at home may or may not be directly related to the home environment. Women report that violence may take place between members of the household or guests; that is friends, acquaintances, other family members or come from total stangers. Violence from strangers in the home took many forms, from obscene and threatening telephone calls, to peeping Toms, to physical and sexual assaults.

And finally, violence in the street and public places may or may not be related to the public environment in the sense that it is that place where strangers meet. The expectation and fear is of attack from strangers, yet disputes also occur between people who know each other. Arguments and assaults between acquaintances, friends or married couples may begin and/or end outside the home or in any public location. We conclude from our evidence that the same types of violence between people may occur in the street, or in the home, or in the workplace, and that *specific violent events are not sealed off into private versus public domains*. We see this as the second major finding of our research.

The women we interviewed, however, defined male violence as a feature of the public rather than the private sphere. The experience of public violence and the fear of public stranger violence in Leeds had a major impact on the women we spoke to. The so-called 'Ripper' murders, and the resulting publicity, intensified feelings of fear and further affected the way women behaved. The 'Ripper' embodied the media image of the random, woman-hating psychopathic killer. The vast majority of women we interviewed were scared and were more frightened than usual of going out at night. Most said they had not always been frightened to do so. Over the previous year the majority of women had restricted their movements in a variety of ways. The most frequent was never to walk alone, followed by changing their mode of transport. Women acquired bikes, cars, used public transport, including taxis, for the first time or more frequently, and women students used the university minibus service provided by the students union (this worked like a taxi service). When not going out alone if possible is combined with never doing so, 83 per cent of the women interviewed were restricted in this way. The 'Ripper' scare did not change behaviour for a substantial minority (18 per cent), however, as they were already not going out alone, or at all, at night.

While these major changes in attitude and behaviour were occurring, the majority of women still regarded the neighbourhood as a safe place to walk around alone in during the day. When asked if the neighbourhood had become more or less safe in the previous twelve months, half said it was about the same even though the question had not offered that option.

The neighbourhood was deliberately not defined by the questionnaire because we wanted to know how the women we interviewed perceived it. From the replies it is possible to work out that its area is approximately a quarter of a mile square. The area consists of quiet residential streets with brief early morning and evening traffic as people go to and return from work. There is a block of little shops and the open space known as the Moor borders one side. The Moor contains a few trees, allotments surrounded by high hedging, and has a gentle slope leading to higher ground in the middle. Because of these factors it is possible to be out of sight of others when walking even though it is a relatively small space. There is no lighting on the Moor and the street lighting is dim as is usual in residential areas. The Moor was a no-go area for women at night even before Peter Sutcliffe began his series of murders.

When asked how the neighbourhood could be made more safe and, later more specifically, if there was anything the police could do, just over half recommended increased police activity, particularly foot patrols, but also changes in police attitudes and a quicker response to calls. Almost a third, however, thought the police could do nothing

A HELPING HAND

either because they were doing all they could or because it might be unwise to have too many police about. The remainder did not know or did not reply. Thus a majority of women think they look to the collective organization of men, that is the police, to protect them from individual male attack. But once attack occurs, the reporting rate is low.

4. Women's views on and experiences of the police

With the help of the local law centre the experiences of women were analysed for the type of crime, if any, that had been committed. The results are presented in Table 8. Table 9 gives a breakdown of the types of minor crimes and their incidence. Where detail was sufficient to establish that an offence had taken place, but not the exact crime, the event was categorized as the lesser crime. While these tables show that most of the experiences of the women interviewed can be seen as crimes, their right to redress through the criminal justice system should not be taken literally. As the experiences of the women who attempted to involve the police show, many of these offences would not be followed up by the police.

With witnessed crime there were fewer major crimes and more unclassifiable incidents than with violence to the interviewed women. These differences probably reflect inadequate observations on the part of the women and possibly relative lack of interest in recounting events. Women suffered ten major crimes; one robbery, three rapes, two indecent assaults, three offences of grievous bodily harm, and one of aggravated bodily harm. The 116 minor crimes were allocated to four categories:

1 indecent exposure
2 obscene and threatening telephone calls
3 assaults, battery, technical battery, breach of the peace, and loitering were classed together
4 insulting or threatening behaviour.

Fifteen events could not be classed as offences either because, like the examples in Chapter 3 (see above, pp. 40–1), no crimes had taken place or there were insufficient details.

Witnessed or overheard crime involved three major offences; a 'Ripper'-like attack and two assaults occasioning actual or grievous

Table 8 *Major–minor crimes to self and other women as defined by criminal law*

	To self			To others			Total	%
	Number of incidents	%	Number of women	Number of incidents	%	Number of women		
Major crimes	10	7	7	3	4	3	13	6
Minor crimes	116	82	89	52	75	39	168	80
No crime and insufficient information to categorize	15	11	14	15	21	11	30	14
Total	141	100	76*	70	100	47*	211	100

* A total of eighty-four women reported incidents. The column totals are less than the sum because some women reported more than one offence.

Table 9   *Types of minor crimes and their incidence*

	To self	%	To others	%	Total	%
Indecent exposure	22	19	—	—	22	13
Obscene or threatening phone calls	13	11	—	—	13	8
Assault, battery, technical battery, breach of peace, loitering	29	25	27	53	56	33
Insulting behaviour or threatening behaviour	52	45	25	47	77	46
Total	116	100	52	100	168	100

bodily harm, one by a husband and the other by a son-in-law. The minor crimes could not involve indecent exposure, because to observe is to experience the incident, and there were no overheard obscene or threatening telephone calls although in theory this is possible. The two latter categories, assault and insulting or threatening behaviour, contain all fifty-two observed minor crimes.

One question raised by the experiences of women with the police is why do they report crimes of violence against them? Even if the act of violence is perceived as a crime the abused woman or witness may prefer to confide solely in her family and friends as did many of those we interviewed. It seems reasonable to assume that to report a crime one must expect to derive some benefit from doing so. This may explain the uneven reporting rates between property theft and damage, and acts of violence experienced by the women we interviewed. Insurance claims depend on reporting property crime and these may be seen as particularly appropriate for police involvement. Of the twenty-three property crimes involving the women we interviewed, a minimum of eleven (48 per cent) and a maximum of nineteen (73 per cent) were reported to the police. (It is unclear whether or not they were reported in eight cases.) These percentages are both far greater than the 13 per cent of crimes of violence reported to the police.

The commonly held view expressed by Sparks, Genn and Dodd (1977, p. 116), 'the victim will presumably not notify the police if *he* regards the incident as too trivial to bother about' (our emphasis), does not explain the experience of the women we interviewed. To recognize an act as threatening, anti-social or hostile, which includes an assessment of the severity of the incident based upon the woman's experience, feelings, and perhaps the response of people whom she cares about, is only the first step in defining an event as a crime against her person. The next step is to define crime according to her understanding of the response of the criminal justice system. She may simply ask herself, 'Is this against the law?'

Our data indicates that women are more likely to base their actions on whether or not they think the police will consider the incident trivial. For example, one woman experienced three incidents, one of which, an indecent exposure, she reported to the police. The other two, an obscene telephone call and an assault (a youth kicked her while she was in a theatre queue), were not reported as she thought they were too trivial. She did, however, report these incidents to us which suggests that she perceived them as hostile acts against her. We suggest that her category, too trivial, is based upon her understanding of the likely response of others, particularly that of the police, to these incidents.

The memory of previous experience with the police will also influence the decision to report other incidents. For example, a 17-year-old woman was raped on two separate occasions but only the first, when she was raped by her uncle, involved the police. She said she felt too ashamed to tell the police as they had not believed her the first time. Her experience was typical of that of many raped women. She was taken to the local hospital for examination where the police were telephoned. She was then taken to the station and questioned for approximately six hours and medically examined further. She said the police told the women who had taken her to hospital that there was proof of rape, but that her uncle had denied it. The police told the woman that there was no proof and that she should let the matter drop for the family's sake. The woman lived with her aunt and uncle and the outcome was that the aunt threw her out of the house. She was living alone in a bedsitting room at the time of our interview. After she moved she asked in a boyfriend who had taken her home one evening. She said he made advances that she resisted but he continued. In the end he physically assaulted and raped her. She again confided in the same friends who saw the young man and told him to leave her alone. Given her previous experience with the police she could see no point in going to them again.

Another example involving a crime legally defined as minor, followed a similar pattern. The woman received a series of obscene telephone calls. He would say, 'Are you alone? . . . Do you masturbate? . . . What do you do in bed?', etc. Sometimes she would hang up, but other times she would shout at him for a while. She said, 'When someone else is in the house it is possible to laugh it off, but I'm often alone. I called the police once, but it was totally useless. They said, "What can we do, people ring up all the time saying this. If it happens a lot we'll send someone around".' Subsequently she experienced two incidents of indecent exposure but she did not report these to the police because of the way they had responded to her earlier request for help.

As women we also accept responsibility for crimes of violence against us. This obviously influences our decisions to report. For example, women who are raped may share the frequently held cultural view that they must have done something to provoke the attack, even when the assailant is a stranger. One woman, an expert in karate, large and physically able expresses it like this:

I was with some men and women friends in a pub and had quite a few drinks. We went to a restaurant. I got fed up with the people I was with and left the restaurant to go home. I decided to cut across a corner of the Moor (a small open space), but would not have gone that way if I hadn't been drinking. Someone came out of the middle of nowhere. He put his hand around my throat from behind and pushed me to the ground. I was saying, 'Don't do this.' I started shouting and he hit me across the face. I was frightened and shut up and then he raped me. He hit me in the chest. I had bruises. Then he got up and ran off leaving me lying there. It was about midnight and muddy and rainy. I had not seen his face. I got up, arranged my clothes and went home, where I took off all my clothes, put them into bag and threw them away the next day. Then I drank some whisky I had in my room. I did not call the police or Rape Crisis and did not mention it to anyone until two weeks later.

[When asked why she had not told anyone she said], Lots of conflicting reasons. I felt guilty. I felt that it was my fault because I had been drinking. I felt angry at myself for not having fought or screamed louder. I thought that I was really strong and that I could fight and was tough. But the violence that was coming from this man really frightened me. He really paralysed me. I didn't care that he had screwed me. It was not the intercourse, not the sex that bothered me as I suppose that I have been willingly raped before, but it was the violence from this man. Now I actually view men with suspicion. All men I see as potential rapists and violent. I have since talked about it to friends who have had similar experiences.

Had this woman been knocked to the ground and had her handbag stolen it is unlikely that she would have had the same feelings of self blame, even if she had been drinking, and she would probably have reported the incident to the police.

For the above reasons we cannot say that women are more likely to report crimes legally defined as major rather than minor. This situation is further complicated because women do not always share the legal view of major and minor crimes. A major crime in law may have a relatively minor effect on the woman who experiences or witnesses it, while a crime legally defined as minor may have a major impact. The example below is of a major crime that had a relatively minor impact on this woman:

I was with a friend coming through the park and we were followed by a group of young blokes, 18-year-olds. They started off by shouting things and we shouted back telling them to leave off. We were feeling very angry at them. Then I got pushed to the ground and they pinched my bag. My friend ripped her dress. We felt really angry and reported it to the police.

Theft with violence is robbery, a major crime. Throughout the interview the woman revealed anger over the incident and a determination to contact the police if she ever saw any of the youths again. She had reported one man earlier who was interviewed but not charged – she presumed through wrong identification. This woman did not admit to or transmit any feelings of fear, or fear that something else might happen, as a result of this experience.

The next example is of a minor crime where the effects have proved long lasting and damaging:

The second night I was home last summer I went to bed at 10 p.m. About 4 a.m. I awoke to find a man crouching by my bed. He touched my hand. I turned over, thinking that it was my mother or my father. I could just see his face against the window. I said, 'Who is it?' He walked out silently. I turned the lights on. I told my parents a man had been in my bedroom. They thought I had a nightmare and didn't believe me. I checked the back door and it was wide open. My mother went out, I thought to tell the police, but to look for footprints to check my story. Then we called the police.

When the police came they told the woman and her parents that the man was a regular, difficult to catch, and related the following history. At 17 he began as a prowler. Now 34 he moved from just prowling, to breaking in and doing nothing, to beginning to touch women's bodies. He found he could put his hands everywhere except their face, hands, and feet without waking them. His stated ultimate desire is to kill a woman slowly and watch her die and he has boasted to the police that he knows the right things to say to psychiatrists. The police concluded that as he has not actually harmed anyone yet, it is difficult to get him.

The police asked this woman if she had been frightened, as that would constitute assault. She replied:

I said I was frightened to be helpful. They asked me if it would have a lasting effect. I said, no, but it has. I get frightened when I am trying to get to sleep. If I hear strange noise, I really believe someone is there. I have to get up and put the light on. Initially I would just lie in bed, unable to move. I was just scared. I put the light on to reassure myself. I made myself do it, otherwise I can't sleep.

But at the time I said it would have no lasting effect. I wasn't very worried you see.

This woman said that the man was prosecuted, but that she did not go to court. Technically this was a minor crime as the man did not break in. The door was unlocked and he did not physically injure her. He may have been detained under the 1959 Mental Health Act, although it is not clear how this could be done or under which section. The lasting effect is that she feels at risk all the time, and particularly vulnerable during the night, as the previously taken for granted safety of her bedroom can no longer be presumed.

It seems that neither the women interviewed nor the police were guided in their actions by the legal distinction between major and minor crime to the extent that might be expected. Table 10 summarizes the offences reported to the police. Only twenty-six offences either experienced or witnessed involved the police. Of the major crimes only the robbery and one rape were reported. Women were more likely to report indecent exposure than any other crime to themselves, including major offences, perhaps because it is a daytime crime. In total 12 per cent of witnessed and experienced violence was reported. As might be expected the proportion reporting violence to the self, 13 per cent, is

Table 10   *Offences reported to the police*

Type of offence	To self	%	To others	%	Proportion of total reported	%
Major	2	20	3	100	$\frac{5}{13}$	38
Minor Indecent exposure	8	38	—	—	$\frac{8}{22}$	38
Obscene or threatening phone calls	1	8	—	—	$\frac{1}{13}$	8
Assault, battery, breach of peace	4	8	3	6	$\frac{7}{56}$	13
Insulting or threatening behaviour	4	5	1	1	$\frac{5}{77}$	6
Proportion of total reported	$\frac{19}{141}$	13	$\frac{7}{70}$	10	$\frac{26}{211}$	12

somewhat greater than that reporting violence to others, 10 per cent. When we look at witnessed crime, however, the distinction between major and minor appears to be operating. All the major assaults to others were reported while very few minor crimes were. Given the low reporting rate overall we conclude that the vast majority of the women interviewed *do not think the police in practice either able or willing to protect them*. We regard this as the third major finding of our survey, and on in keeping with the facts of police activity in response to requests for help from women (Pahl 1983).

If we look at what the police do by examining first the major offences and then the minor that were reported to them, we see a pattern of minimal intervention, i.e. very little action is taken. The two major crimes directly experienced by women that were reported, the robbery and the rape, have been described. The three major crimes that were witnessed were all physical attacks. In the two assaults that took place at home the women turned to neighbours for help. In one the woman left before the police arrived, while in the other the police tried to get the woman to charge her husband rather than do so themselves. Although the police have legal power to bring prosecutions in all crimes they usually do not do so in so-called domestic disputes. The police do not arrest the man or take any action except perhaps to move him temporarily on. They tell the woman that it is her responsibility to prosecute, which in this case, as in many others, she did not do. A woman may not want to press charges for many reasons, not least being that her attacker will be out on remand until the case comes up which could be months. The wide discretionary power possessed by the police is not common knowledge and is rarely challenged.

The third reported incident was an assault in the street. The woman who witnessed the attack along with a male friend, turned a corner and saw a woman lying on the pavement as a man fled. Her friend went to telephone the police while she stayed with the unconscious woman. She reports:

The police came in fifteen to twenty minutes. One policeman asked my male friend some questions and took his address. I asked if he wanted mine which he took down reluctantly, and improperly, as I later found out. The woman was taken away by ambulance and the police let us go home but they turned up at 3 a.m. saying that the first policeman should not have let us leave the scene of the incident. They said they didn't know as yet if the attack was connected to others in the area, but it seemed likely. They left saying, 'If we decide to treat this incident seriously, we may interview you again.' Three weeks later Jacqueline Hill [the thirteenth victim of Peter Sutcliffe, the so-called 'Ripper'] was murdered in what seemed to me to be rather similar circumstances, i.e., not very late at night, a student, just off a main, well-lit road, hit on the back of the head, etc. The *Yorkshire Post* reported that the police said the attack I witnessed was not connected to other incidents in the area, but when the 'Ripper' squad was increased, they said the case was 'being reviewed'. I never heard anything more, but Peter Sutcliffe [subsequently found guilty] has not been charged with this assault. However, I believe that this was a 'Ripper' attack and that if the police had decided to treat the incident seriously Jacqueline Hill's murder might have been prevented. I should like this to be public knowledge.

Of the twenty-one minor crimes reported, the police answered all but one call, although they were not always prompt. This enabled several offenders to get away. The most common outcome was that after the police listened to the woman's account either at her home or at the station, she heard nothing more. In several incidents it is clear that something must have been noted in writing as the police returned at a later time. Women reported that a man was caught and charged in only two incidents; the prowler discussed earlier, and a notorious rapist known as the Chapeltown rapist. A woman interrupted him by coming in the front door before he attacked another woman living in the house. As he had done nothing, this, too, was a minor crime. Only 8 per cent of reported crime led to an arrest, so far as our respondents knew, and none involved a major crime. The conclusion we draw from these experiences is that *women are much more likely than the police to perceive violence to themselves as serious*. While this finding is commonsense, the discrepancy is greater than many readers realize. We regard this as our fourth major finding.

We asked two questions about satisfaction with police action. Table 11 presents the views of women who reported on violence. With respect to violence to the self, neither of the two women who reported major crimes were satisfied. Of the three witnessed major crimes, one of the women was satisfied with the action of the police. Regarding minor crimes, approximately half were satisfied in both groups.

The recent major study on satisfaction with police and court action shows that dissatisfaction increases as the case is processed through the

Table 11   *Satisfaction with police action – violence reported within past year*

Satisfaction	Violence to self				Violence to others					
	Major crimes	*%*	*Minor crimes*	*%*	*Major crimes*	*%*	*Minor crimes*	*%*	*Total*	*%*
Satisfied	—	—	9	53	1	33	1	25	11	42
Not satisfied	2	100	8	47	2	67	1	25	13	50
Left before police arrived	—	—	—	—	—	—	2	50	2	8
Total	2	100	17	100	3	100	4	100	26	100

criminal justice system (Shapland, Willmore and Duff 1981). Satisfaction is highest after the first interview with the police. They took their survey sample from police records, thus only those individuals the police had already decided to treat seriously were questioned, unlike our study. This probably explains the higher rate of satisfaction found by Joanna Shapland *et al*.

Table 12 reports on the last contact women had with the police whatever the offence or help they requested. The table shows that satisfaction increases when considering police action around other types of offences. Just over two-thirds liked the way the police dealt with property offences and all were satisfied with their intervention in non-criminal incidents, like a missing dog.

Table 12   *Satisfaction with police action – last contact initiated by woman and/or others on her behalf*

Satisfaction	Burglary and theft of own and others property	%	Other misc. (e.g., missing dog)	%	Violence to women	%
Satisfied	28	70	6	100	10	40
Not satisfied	10	25	—	—	13	52
No answer or not applicable	2	5	—	—	2	8
Total	40	100	6	100	25	100

Of the total interviewed, seventy-one women (55 per cent) had initiated contact with the police on behalf of themselves or others at some time in the past. If we include the views of women who were contacted initially by the police, rather than the other way around, there is even less satisfaction with their actions. A surprisingly small number of women had never been in touch with the police (20 per cent).

Three complaints about police action stand out; not responding quickly enough to calls, not knowing the outcome of complaints, and the lack of seriousness with which the complaint was treated. Women were anxious that they should be taken seriously and be dealt with in a sympathetic manner. One woman, reporting an indecent exposure, said the police searched the streets and although the offender was not found, 'I was much comforted and calmed by their [the police] behaviour. I was not made to feel it was a trivial incident or a waste of their time. The seriousness with which it was handled was most important.' Another woman reporting the same offence was dissatisfied. 'They were not bothered, very disinterested. They took a statement and followed it up two months later with a visit from the vice squad. They wanted a better description. They asked if he had a beard.' The implication was that the incident was followed up because bearded Peter Sutcliffe had been arrested. The woman was indignant because her experience was not treated with concern. Interest was shown only when it might be linked to a major crime.

While there were a number of indecent exposure offences within a small geographical area, none of the offenders were apprehended so far as the women knew. For example, one woman said that the man who had exposed himself to her could be identified easily as he 'had a big belly, funny hat and limps'. Upon recounting the incident it emerged that two of her friends had also seen this man but so far as she knew the police had not picked him up. Satisfaction with police action did not depend on their catching and prosecuting offenders. Many women thought that would be expecting too much. 'What can the police do?' 'They are doing as much as they can.' These two comments made by a small number of women typifies this attitude. Another way of interpreting this type of comment is that male violence to woman is not seen as contestable.

The experiences of the women we interviewed can only lead to our fifth major finding; that *the police do not interfere in any serious way with male violence to women.* The police can be likened to gatekeepers,

standing between abused women and violent men, severely rationing the numbers of these men to be prosecuted. This is true even if police action (or lack of it) only reflects accurately what they know would happen if more cases went to court; that is, nothing or next to nothing. The police are not necessarily being hostile in not enforcing the criminal law in relation to abused women.

By looking at how women define violent events in relation to their actual experiences and the responses of the police, we can begin to cast some light both on why women expect and seek protection from men, the abusing group, and also how male violence to women is socially constructed to perpetuate itself. But before we draw all these threads together, we will briefly summarize the major divisions within the criminal law to show that appropriate legislation exists, and that the greater problem is discriminatory enforcement.

5. Their law: some basic information

The criminal justice system divides violence into two categories; violence against the person and sexual offences.

Violence against the person

This category includes a variety of crimes that result in the death of a person or endanger life. These crimes may be specific to children or adults or may specify the means by which the crime takes place, for example possession of firearms or placing objects on railway lines. The major categories are murder, attempted murder and threat or conspiracy to commit murder, manslaughter, infanticide, wounding and other acts that endanger life. Lesser categories include wounding that harms but does not endanger life, assault, a variety of offences harmful to children (cruelty, abandonment, stealing, concealment of birth), and procuring an illegal abortion.

The Offences Against the Person Act of 1861 is the most frequently used legislation for assault and wounding offences. The least serious offence under this Act is common assault. The court in which a crime is processed has an effect upon the maximum possible sentence, since Crown courts are empowered to give longer sentences than the magistrates for some crimes. For example, if common assault is tried in a magistrates court the maximum sentence is six months while in a Crown court it is one year.

The next most serious offence under the 1861 Act is actual bodily harm (ABH). The maximum sentence is five years if tried in a Crown court and six months in a magistrates court. Under the Act, ABH can be an injury from a slight bruise to quite severe injury, although in practice injuries tend to be the more severe.

Serious wounding can occur with or without intent to harm another person. Different sections of the Act are used depending on whether or not the prosecution thinks intent can be proved. Wounding with intent to cause grievous bodily harm (GBH) has a maximum sentence of life imprisonment. When specific intent cannot be proved, it is necessary to show that the injury was caused by a person willingly or recklessly. Thus, if you hit someone with an iron bar and fracture their skull while shouting 'I'm going to break your head in', the verbal statement directly indicates intent. If you do the same act silently, specific intent cannot be proved unless you hit the person repeatedly, and a different section of the Act with a lesser penalty will be used. These offences are tried in the Crown court.

In the past century the 1861 Act has been amended by the Criminal Justice Act of 1925 and the Criminal Law Act of 1977. Common assault, ABH and GBH are frequent charges brought against men who violently assault women. The sentence will depend upon previous convictions and the specific circumstances. We do not have the necessary information on differential sentencing, but it is thought that lesser sentences are given when the victim and offender know each other than when they do not. Conditional and suspended sentences, fines and probation are a more likely outcome than a prison sentence for crimes categorized as less serious. Within the criminal justice system the definition of 'less serious' has both legal and social components.

Sexual offences

Sexual offences may be specific to children or adults, to males or females and specify particular types of behaviour. The major categories are buggery, indecent assault, indecency between males, rape, unlawful intercourse with a girl under 13 and under 16 years, incest, procuration, abduction, bigamy, soliciting by a man, and gross indecency with a child.

Consent may be a legal defence as in rape, or irrelevant, as in incest. By and large children cannot be deemed to have consented to sexual acts. It is sufficient to establish that the offender committed the offence for conviction. When consent is a defence, the defendant must also prove that she did not consent. Sexual offences also are categorized as crimes against the person; and there is the same reluctance to bring prosecutions.

There are three legally defined offences where the victim is always a male; buggery, indecent assault on a male, and indecency between males. Offences against females include rape, indecent assault, unlawful intercourse with a girl under 13, unlawful intercourse with a girl 13 to 16, incest, and abduction. Offences against males or females are procuration, bigamy, gross indecency with a child, and soliciting by a man.

Maximum sentences are sex and age specific for indecent assault, ten years if the victim is a male, five years if the victim is a female child under 13 years, and two years if a female over 13 years of age. This is one of the areas of proposed change in the current reconsideration of sexual offences. Thus far, the Criminal Law Revision Committee has issued a working paper for discussion by the public on the age of consent and the offences of non-consensual buggery, indecent assault, incest, and rape in marriage (1980). The Home Office utilizes these categories in the annual presentation of statistical data on interpersonal crime.

6. Fitting the pieces together: violence and the public–private divide

Male violence to women is enclosed within a circular system. We are able to describe this by a diagram (Figure 1) in a series of steps that return to reinforce the starting point.

1   Fear of violence in public places is fed by the media, informal rumour, personal experience of people known to us, and our own experience. The public world is seen as the place of strangers who may not share our values about appropriate social behaviour. Women are expected to be more careful in their public behaviour than men and when attacks occur are often held at least partially responsible for them. Women's fear of public abuse is socially sanctioned and increases belief that the home is (or should be) a safe place.

2   Fear of violence in public places leads to a lessening of public participation by women. This can be total if they decide never to go out alone, or partial if they go out less often. Each woman works out, possibly only semi-consciously, the places, times and means governing her use of public space. For example, a woman may not feel able to use the local public open space, even during the day (except to walk across), unless someone is with her, who can be a child as well as another adult. She may feel she can enter some pubs on her own but not others, or some with other women but not others, or some only with a male escort. It is not a simple matter of being able to go anywhere during the day but being highly restricted during the hours of night.

3   No matter how variable a woman's response, restrictions on public access result in greater dependency on the protection of men both as escorts and in a more general sense. The pressure from the outside, or public world, creates a feeling of dependency that helps to structure an actual dependence of women on men in their home. Dependence of women on particular men is, of course, furthered by other social structural factors. Economic dependence on the wages of men and state

1. fear of abuse or attack from strange men (through media, own experience, and that of others) increases belief in safety at home

which reinforces

which reinforces

6. if a woman sees the police as inappropriate or unhelpful and does not turn to them— nothing happens

5. if a woman goes to the police, nothing happens

2. leads to restrictions on when and how we go out, particularly at night

going out less often   not going out alone

3. this fear results in greater dependency on individual male 'protection' as escorts and at home

4. dependency on men creates conditions where it is easier for an individual male to assault a woman he knows without fear of retaliation from her

if approached medical and social work services reinforce expectations and experience that no one can/will help

women's culturally defined responsibility for male violence increases with the closeness of the relationship

The perpetuation of the division between the public and private sphere of women's lives

support for the social organization and maintenance of the nuclear family, for example, through housing policies, the various systems of state benefit, including income tax allowances and assessment, are of particular importance.

4   Dependence on the men with whom women live creates the conditions where it is easier for individual men to assault 'their women' secure in the knowledge that they cannot retaliate easily. Men's behaviour is supported by a general cultural understanding that defines women as responsible for male violence, and this responsibility

increases with the closeness of the relationship. If women attempt to object by turning to state agencies, the response of the medical and social work services is, by and large, to reinforce expectations and experiences that no one can or will help. The problem of male violence is turned back upon the woman who becomes labelled inadequate or deviant (Stark, Flitcraft, Frazier 1979; Maynard forthcoming).

5   Our study illustrates that if women reach out to the criminal justice system – the police – nothing happens, or nothing happens that women can understand as the result of their actions. If men are penalized for their crimes it occurs in some obscure way, divorced from the active participation of women in curtailing the violence of particular men. This encourages dependence on the collective male protection system which has the effect of reinforcing a state of dependent helplessness. It does not reduce women's fear of public violence. If women decide the police will not or cannot help, or that it is inappropriate to involve them, fear of public abuse remains unchallenged.

1   We have now completed the circle and are back to no. 1. Unchallenged public abuse reinforces fear as nothing stands between women and attack by unknown men in public places except the careful monitoring of access and the means by which this is to be accomplished. And around the circle we go again.

But other pressures make it necessary for women to go out at times and in ways that they may think inappropriate. As we have discussed, many women work in situations where harassment is part of the job, or must do night shifts, or attempt to work in or train for employment defined as male. This necessity to go out is a constant reminder of vulnerability. As women we cannot relax our vigilance, and this serves to remind us that we are tolerated in these settings on certain conditions. The need for male protection is reiterated in the deepest layers of ourselves.

During the five years that the so-called 'Ripper' roamed the North, the consciousness of women began to be transformed. Women began to call on women to depend on each other and not men. The widespread rumour that the 'Ripper' was a policeman, along with the police's inability to capture him, began to invalidate the belief that the collective male system, the criminal justice system, provides protection for women. In our study women recognized the part groups of women had played in helping survivors of violence and made suggestions for the

'No, Madam. We're not standing here in case the Ripper comes along. We're trying to catch these dreadful spray painters.'

extension of voluntary and self-help organizations such as rape crisis, self-defence groups, safe house programmes, advice centres for women, neighbourhood and women's groups, and escort and transport services. Three-quarters of the women we interviewed had heard of the major groups working against violence to women in the Leeds area; that is, Women's Aid, Rape Crisis, and Women Against Violence Against Women, although fewer knew how to contact these organizations if needed.

The feminist response to violence from men is that women should develop ways of depending on each other for protection. Women should accompany each other when out at night and set up women-operated transport systems. This demand is radical because it is not based on deference to and dependence on men. On the contrary, the aim is to break the connection. When the demand for a curfew on men first surfaced it was met with shock and disbelief, so strong is the system of dependence and male privilege. Yet curfews on men do occur in some situations when the state decides it is in its interests. For example, many young blacks had to be indoors at night after the Moss Side riots, as a condition of bail. A curfew on all men after dark would make the streets safe for women.

Force and its threat is used to maintain power differences over many oppressed and exploited groups, including particular social classes, races, and countries. The maintenance of power differences between men and women is no exception, but each system has its own specific forms to be analysed. The division of women's lives into public and private spheres is central to the process of ensuring dependence on men both as individuals and collectively, and the greater the threat of attack, the more intense this is, thus ensuring the perpetuation of the system.

Social systems, however, can be challenged and changed. The process begins with transformations of consciousness generated by our experiences of the real world. The exceptional conditions arising from the 'Ripper's' reign of terror, by exposing the contradiction in depending upon men, the abusing group, for protection, has played an important role in fueling a demand for an end to male violence to women. The process of challenge and change has begun.

Information gathering has a particular role to play in transforming consciousness. In the next chapter we provide practical suggestions for feminist groups who want to undertake further research on violence to women.

FITTING THE PIECES TOGETHER

the law and response of police

women do not think police able or willing to help them, —nor were they

actual experiences

specific types of violent events are not sealed off into private versus public places

how women define violent events

women define violence by how frightened or out of control of the situation they are and believe themselves to be. The more uncertainty about the outcome, the more terrifying the encounter

7. Planning your questionnaire: practical help

While we were interviewing a number of questions were raised by the answers women gave us. We were not then living in the area and a better local knowledge would have assisted us when compiling our questionnaire. Some of the points touched upon by the women we interviewed are expanded here. We recommend that the structure of your questionnaire follows ours, while incorporating the suggestions outlined below.

Detailed questions on the area (Our Question 1, see pp. 80–5 for our questionnaire and incident sheet.)

Any community study must necessarily pay particular attention to the characteristics of the area to be surveyed. Some aspects will be unique to the area. We suggest that you tour your area looking for:

1 Location of passages, alleyways, footpaths.
2 Location of common ground, waste ground, playing fields, leisure parks, odd grassy spaces.
3 Location of rubbish tips, derelict houses, garages, factories, building sites.

You will need to know about street lighting:

1   Where are lamps sited?
2   Are they in good working order?
3   Are some streets more dimly lit than others?

You will need to know the location of:

1   High hedges or bushes.
2   High walls or fences.

Make a list of those aspects that you think may restrict the access women in your area have to public places. You will probably find it useful to begin the interview with a more open ended question about the general safety of the neighbourhood during the day and night as we did in Questions 1f, 1g and 1h (see our questionnaire on pages 80–5). After a woman has answered the general question(s), then ask her about each point on the checklist. For example, 'How do you feel about walking by the factory on . . . . Street during the day? After dark?'

It could be useful to obtain information about telephone access. Some suggested questions are listed below.

1 Do you have a telephone in your home?

2 (If in flats or multi-occupied accommodation) Do you have access to a telephone in your house?

3 Where is the nearest public call box from your home?

4 Is the telephone usually in good working order?

5 How long does it usually take for repair work to be carried out?

You may think it relevant to ask about the availability and use of public transport (buses, trains, taxis) and private transport (cars, bicycles, etc.).

Experiences of witnessed violence to others, in neighbourhood and elsewhere (Our Questions 2 and 3)

Questions on witnessed violence provide an important cross-check on information gained about violence to the woman herself. Women report seeing other women being beaten by their husbands or boyfriends while the women being attacked may not wish to talk about men they know or are related to. It also enables women to talk about their own experiences in the third person. We did not include questions on violence between men, but women did mention this as Sandra McNeill found when interviewing. It might be useful to include questions such as:

1 Have you seen a fight between men during the past twelve months?

2 Where did this incident occur?

3 Did you know any of the men involved?

4 What happened?

5 How did this make you feel?

6 Do you think it has affected your behaviour in any way? How?

Experiences to self (Our Questions 4, 5, 6 and 7)

Question 6 in our questionnaire is about sexual harassment. We did not specifically mention sexual harassment *at work*. In the light of a growing awareness about sexual harassment in the workplace you may wish to include a complete block on this question. For example:

1   Do men at work take it for granted that they can behave in a familiar way with you?
>   your boss
>   workmates
>   general public/clients

2   Do you know if your union is involved in any action to combat sexual harassment at work? If so, what?

3   Would you support action taken by women to highlight these problems? If yes, what actions would you support?

Pornography

On reflection, the major gaps in our questionnaire were in relation to pornography, that is the representation of sexual violence and sexual exploitation of women. You might have a series of questions that tackle pornography both in the local neighbourhood and the town. For example, you could look at the magazines sold by local newsagents. You might ask:

1   Do you know that . . . . sells *Penthouse, Playboy*, another?

2   Do you think that this kind of magazine should be sold in a newsagents which is regularly used by women and children?

3   Would you support action taken by local women to persuade . . . . to stop selling this material?

The location of sex shops could be looked at and the following questions asked:

1   Do you know that there is a sex shop in . . . . Street?
2   Do you know what they sell?
3   Would you support local women taking action to get this shop closed? If yes, what type of action?

You could also look for anti-women films on show either locally or in town. You might ask:

1   Do you know that the film 'Blood, Lust and Gore' is coming to the Roxy in . . . . Street?
2   Will you go and see it?
3   What do you think about films that show women as victims of sex and violence?
4   Do you think these kinds of films make men more violent in their behaviour to women?
5   Did you know that research in Canada and Britain shows that men after seeing films which are sexually violent behave in a more violent way towards women?
6   How do these kinds of films make you feel?
7   Would you support action taken by local women to stop the showing of such films in our cinemas? If yes, what actions would you support?

An investigation into the feelings of women, particularly elderly and housebound women, on the television programmes available was suggested. Many complained to interviewers about being subjected to unacceptable levels of violence in the programmes shown (see above, p. 18). It seems that for these women the fear of violence from the outside is reinforced by the television inside. The following are examples of questions that might be asked:

1   Do you think that the amount of sex and violence shown in television programmes is reasonable?
2   If not, which programmes do you object to most? How do these make you feel?
3   Would you support a protest by women to the television broadcasting company? If yes, what action would you support?

You may wish to repeat Question 5 about the relationship between violence in films and increasing male violence (above, in the section on pornography). Many families now have videos in their homes, which often means that they also have pornography. Pornography is now available for all the family because censorship restrictions are not enforceable once the cassette is inside the home. You could look for the places where videos are sold in the neighbourhood and town and check the titles and contents for sexual and other violence to women. The following questions could be asked:

1   Do you have a video in your home?
2   Who decided to get one?
3   What kinds of films do you hire/buy?
4   Where do you hire/buy your cassettes?
5   Do you or any other member of your household watch films showing sexual violence to women? If yes, which films are these?

6   Do you think that video films which show sexual violence to women should be available to the general public?
7   Would you support women taking action to prevent the sale of offensive material? If so, what action?

Contact with the police and other agencies (Our Questions 7 and 8)

Another cross-check relates to satisfaction with the police and reporting rates. You will see that our Question 7 is about damage to property. This question was based on our personal experience as women and also as workers in Women's Aid. This experience has shown us that when a man cannot get at the woman he wishes to hurt and injure he may take revenge on property either owned or used by her. We have seen women's homes and possessions smashed because the women have removed themselves from violent homes. While we had one incident of this type reported to us, many more women told us about property theft, both burglary and damage to or theft of cars, bicycles and other property left outside their homes. The answers to this question, together with Question 8, gave us another two important checks on our information.

1   It showed that the women we interviewed did report crimes to the police if they felt the police could and would be of some help.
2   It enabled us to compare the reporting, handling and satisfaction rates of property theft with personal violence.

Question 8 also enabled us to pick up anything that we may have previously missed about women's contact with the police. If you are particularly interested in the behaviour of the police in your area you might expand this question to obtain more detailed information. For example, if police harassment of prostitutes is prevalent in the area you could gather details about this.

How to make the neighbourhood safer (Our Question 9)

This question was a bit of a non-starter in that women rarely managed to think of ways in which the neighbourhood could be made safer. Women would mainly suggest more policemen on foot patrols. Their attitude should not be seen as lacking imagination, but rather further endorsing the circular process shown in Figure 1 (above, p. 66).

If you are thinking of taking some action based on the results of the survey you might ask if women would be willing to become involved. Or if you want to get support for a women's centre, a refuge for battered women, or a rape crisis centre, this is probably the right place in the questionnaire to ask for it. If a woman has a private telephone you may wish to act on a suggestion of Sandra's and co-ordinate a telephone link-up scheme.

Women's organizations (Our Question 10)

This is a very useful question for two reasons. First, it enables you to check how effectively information is received about the existence and purpose of women's organizations, such as Women's Aid and Rape Crisis. Second, it creates a space in the questionnaire where you can talk about women taking action against male violence and to offer leaflets explaining in more detail the function of such groups.

Women's living situations (Our Question 11)

In an effort to find out more about the lives of the women we asked if they lived with anyone. This was intended to refer to adult partners. We then asked about children and their whereabouts. We asked how long women had lived in the neighbourhood, which enabled us to distinguish between long-standing and more recent members of the community. On reflection we should have followed up this question by asking why they had moved. This might have given us more information on violence in the home (see above, p. 22).

We asked if others lived in the house as a way of checking on how many women actually lived in the area of the survey and so that we knew who to interview. By knowing how many women there are it is possible to work out the percentage interviewed. In a multi-occupied area with rapid turnover this can be difficult; for example, we were never able to say exactly how many women lived in our seven streets although we know we contacted most of them. This is important because there may be something special about women who are hard to contact, and this cannot be disproved unless everyone is reached. In general, the more information you are able to gain the greater your understanding will be of violence in the lives of women.

We mentioned (see above, p. 15) that we estimated the ages of women, but it would be better to ask directly. Age is used to divide women as we are led to believe that our interests and vulnerabilities change with time. Women's Aid, Rape Crisis and Incest Survivors provide evidence to the contrary. If your information on age is systematic and accurate, you will be able to compare types of violence, and other information, with it.

It would be useful to know if a woman is in paid employment. This information will come out if you ask specifically about sexual harassment at work. You can then ask about the type of employment, if that is not clear. If you are in an area of high unemployment (most areas fall into this category now), you may wish to include a section specifically on women's paid work. Information on the particular position of women in the labour market could be used to seek funds from the Equal Opportunities Commission, the Manpower Services Commission or some other local or central government scheme to relieve women's unemployment.

Incident sheet

The incident sheet is self-explanatory, but just a reminder of the point made on p. 27. Fill in the questionnaire first and leave the incident sheet(s) to the last.

Repeated interviewing

It seems likely that had we interviewed women more than once we would have obtained even more information. Repeated interviewing gives a greater chance of establishing a relationship of mutual trust between the woman being interviewed and the interviewer. For example, one woman interviewed completed the questionnaire with no incidents being reported. Then as a throw-away remark she mentioned being attacked and threatened at work. She was an officer with the DHSS and saw this as a part of the job. She thought women officers were probably more vulnerable to attack than men. A week later Sheila called back to interview a woman living upstairs who was out when she paid her first call. This woman was out again, but the woman she interviewed the week before came to the door to say 'hello' and to ask how she was getting on. After chatting for a while she quite casually told Sheila of a very violent episode between herself and a former boyfriend that had taken place the previous year. She had made no mention of this during the first visit. Giving women time to think about the questions and the meaning of violence in their lives might lead to a greater yielding of information. We did not do this because of the amount of time we had to do the study. One approach would be to re-interview a proportion of the initial group. However, they would need to be chosen in a random way; that is, every woman should have an equal chance of being re-interviewed. For example, you might choose every tenth house or throw all the addresses in a hat and draw out a certain number.

A last general point

Devising a questionnaire is very important in that the questions asked will to some extent influence the answers given. Therefore, the first aim must be to minimize this control and maximize the information receiving process. Because there is a tendency to agree with suggestions contained within questions you should try to avoid putting words in the woman's mouth. But however well constructed, it is not possible to gather all the information on violence to women in any given area, nor is it possible to know the proportion gained. What is possible is to systematically gather information that tells us more about how violence from men controls our environment and limits our freedom within it.

The questionnaire and incident sheet used in the Leeds study

1   The 'Ripper' murders and the recent coverage given to them in the newspapers and on the television made many women frightened. How did it affect you?

   a   Were you scared?
   b   Did it make you restrict your usual movements at all?
   c   If yes, in what ways have your movements changed? (places, persons accompanying, mode of transport)

d If you did go out alone at night were you more frightened than usual?

e Are you frightened to go out alone at night?

f Do you think that this neighbourhood is a safe place to walk around alone?
  i during the daytime
  ii after dark

g Do you think that during the last twelve months the neighbourhood has:
  i become safer
  ii become less safe

h Explain in what ways the neighbourhood has become safer or less safe.

2 Have you heard or seen any women being threatened in the neighbourhood during the past year?

a While leaving or coming home.
b During an argument or quarrel.
c While out with other people.
d Any other.

If yes, fill in first attached incident sheet.

3 Have you seen any woman being threatened anywhere else in Leeds during the past year?

a In the street.
b In a pub or other public place.
c In her or someone else's home.
d Any other.

If yes, fill in second attached incident sheet.

4 Has anyone threatened you in any way in the past year?

a Someone you know.
b A member of your family.
c A friend.
d A neighbour.
e Acquaintance.
f Stranger.

If yes, fill in third attached incident sheet.

5   Within the past year have you been in any situation in which violence has been used against you?

   a In an argument or a quarrel?
   b Did anyone physically attack or assault you in any way?
   c Did anyone hit you, or use any other kind of violence against you?
   d Did anyone try to attack you, or assault you, or molest you in any way?
   e Anyone at all – even someone close to you?

If yes, fill in fourth attached incident sheet.

6   Have you faced any sexual harassment during the past year?

   a Rape.
   b Sexual assault.
   c Sexual attack.
   d Indecent suggestions.
   e Indecent exposure (flashing).
   f Obscene phone calls.

If yes, fill in fifth attached incident sheet if different incident from Questions 4 or 5.

7   Has anyone deliberately damaged any property belonging to you during the past year?

   a A window in your house/flat.
   b Car, bicycle.
   c Any other.

If yes, fill in sixth incident sheet if different incident from Questions 4, 5 or 6.

7A Do these situations make you think of anything else that has happened to women during the past year in Leeds as a result of all the publicity about violence to women?

8 When did you last have any contact with the police?

    a What were the circumstances?
    b Were you satisfied with their behaviour on that occasion?
    c If the answer is no give reasons.

9 What do you think could be done to make this neighbourhood safer?

    a Is there anything the police could do?
    b If the answer is yes, then what could they do?
    c Do you think that any official people could be more helpful, for example.
        i   councillors;
        ii social workers;
        iii others.
    d What do you think that they could do?
    e Do you think that voluntary or self-help organizations can help?
    f If yes then how?

10 Have you heard of any organizations that help women who are being threatened or attacked by men?

    a Women's Aid
    b Rape Crisis
    c Women Against Violence Against Women
    d Others
    e Would you know how to contact any of the women's organizations should you or anyone else need them? Explain where you would contact them.

11 Do you live with anyone? – husband, boyfriend, girlfriend, other.

    a Do you have any children?
    b How many of them live with you?
    c If not all of your children live with you, where are they?
    d How long have you lived in this neighbourhood?
    e Are there other people living in this house?
    f Do any other women live here?

g   If yes, how many and when do you think that they would be home for us to interview them?

Incident sheet

1   Describe the incident – what exactly did he/they do to you?

2   Who was involved – explain their connection to you?

3   State as near as possible when this happened?

a   month. . . . year. . . .
b   time: day. . . . night. . . .

4   Describe where the incident took place

a   home
b   someone else's home
c   pub or other public place
d   street – exact location on street, i.e., state landmarks, buildings etc.

5   Where or whom did you turn to for help?

6   If you did not tell anyone at the time of the incident occurring then explain?

7   What was the final outcome of the incident – explain?

8   Do you think that this was what should have happened – if not explain what you think ought to have happened – or what you would have like to have seen happen?

9   State extent of injuries you sustained.

10   Did you see a doctor?

11   State name and address of doctor.

12   Was this your usual doctor?

13 What did he/she say to you and how did he/she treat you?

14 If you went to hospital, state which one.

15 How did the hospital staff behave towards you? What did they say?

16 If you were admitted to hospital, state dates from. . . . to. . . .

17 Have you suffered any permanent damage as a result of your injuries?

18 If yes, give details.

19 Have you received any compensation?

20 If yes, give

    a   details of case.
    b   name of lawyer.
    c   relevant dates.

8. Positive proposals for research from Women's Aid Federation England

Women's Aid has a decade of experience of violence to women. Flowing from this are a series of questions the Women's Aid Federation England believe could be examined to further the interests of all women and which they raised in a paper presented at the DHSS Conference on Violence in the Family, 28–30 September 1981, entitled 'Violence to Women in the Home: A Research Strategy'. The conference was called to publicize the results of approximately £300,000 spent by the DHSS on research into violence in marriage, and was attended by high-ranking public officials and professionals. You will see from the following how little the research actually tackled and how much might usefully be done.

Positive proposals for research

Effects of violence in the home on women and the state response

The effects of violence in the home on women have largely been ignored as an area of research. In our experience, these effects may include both temporary and permanent personality damage as well as physical impairment. Women may be prescribed mind altering drugs as out-patients, admitted to a mental hospital, attempt suicide, or achieve it. Women may also be murdered. Strategies to lessen, if not eliminate, the effects of violence on women can only be based on a thorough understanding of the psycho-social processes involved. Women often respond to violence against them by assuming responsibility for the attacks. This outcome should not be regarded as natural, but as an area for investigation. Less frequently women respond to violence by attacking others, and this too needs investigation. We propose studies in the following areas:

Authority and obedience

While some women find the violence directed at them to be unanticipated, others report that, as long as the men with whom they live are not challenged or disobeyed, no abuse occurs or it is limited. As is true of oppressed people generally, women who live with violent men study their behaviour closely in order to be able to avoid violent encounters. We need to know more about the limits women set on their behaviour and their understanding about the 'rules' men set for them. These restrictions and behavioural demands can become intolerable and therefore break down. We need to know more about the conditions under which rebellion occurs. This material should be examined in relation to the concepts of authority and obedience.

Torture and dependency

We find a tendency in the work already published to limit inquiry into the effects of battering to a catalogue of the more obvious short-term physical aspects. This was the type of evidence that was initially required to confront the public conscience as women's indignation about battering surfaced into a demand for action. This need remains but it is insufficient for a full appreciation of the consequences of domestic violence.

1   The immediate, obvious physical suffering of the women who come into Women's Aid refuges can be horrific in its extent and severity, and some women will always bear the scars of injury on their bodies. However, we are also concerned that further consideration should be given both to the lasting effects of more general physical damage, and to the short- and long-term effects of emotional and mental suffering. From our experience within refuges, and in our follow-up work among single parent families, we see a parallel between, on the one hand, the short- and long-term effects of violence in the home and, on the other, the effects of torture on prisoners. Diana Russell in her study of rape in marriage in the US (1982) has begun an examination of the literature on torture for its relevance in understanding the effects on women of their abuse in the home. This is likely to be a fruitful approach that needs to be pursued.

2   Researchers are failing to recognize the full range of the psycho-social effects of battering and the long-term nature of these. The constant pressures of the violent situation are debilitating; the experience of fear, pain, confusion and humiliation leads to a paralysis which is not easily shed. Beyond the initial confusion, apathy or despair of women coming into the refuge, we note a continuing loss of confidence, energies and initiative, and inability to cope with official-dom and authoritarian personalities, and difficulty in making decisions. A high emotional involvement with the past appears to remain as a long-term problem which becomes overlaid with the difficulties and tensions of new and increased responsibilities, poverty and isolation.

3   We need to study battered women who return to violent men by exploring the ways the experience of violence reinforces the dependence already imposed upon women by the economic and social structures and reinforced by socialization. We feel that there is little or no recognition of the interaction between socially constructed dependence and the further powerlessness experienced by women who are battered in their homes. Thus, there is little or no appreciation of the mental and emotional suffering of battered women created by a society which recognizes and values women only for their service to men and as good

mothers. This devaluation of women as people in their own right adds to the experience of battering the stigma of failure.

4 We should look again at the responsibility for children that women assume, and which society expects of them, especially in relation to the creation and maintenance of dependence of women on men. Dependence is the most powerful factor in keeping women within a violent situation, in taking them back there, and in preventing the development of independence in women.

The health and medical treatment of battered women

There has been very little work on the general health of battered women, either the short- or long-term aspects, although several researchers have indicated that physical and mental health problems seem high. For instance, in the Welsh Women's Aid study of the employment position of women who had been through their refuges, of the 51 per cent of the women interviewed who reported health problems, 32 per cent said these were due to battering and 19 per cent described themselves as having 'nervous disorders' (Welsh Women's Aid 1981).

To gain information on women's health it is important that the right questions are asked and that replies are interpreted with more understanding and fewer assumptions. An example of shortcomings in this respect may be found in a DHSS survey of single parents on Family Income Supplement (DHSS 1979). Here the higher proportion of women than men in the sample who reported health problems was apparently not seen as a matter worth pursuing, indeed it was considered merely to be a possible indication that women feel freer to complain about their health than men. Our experience in Women's Aid confirms that ill health is frequent.

One well-travelled individual progression is from abuse to the prescription of tranquillizers or anti-depressants and then to mental hospital admission and/or attempted and achieved suicide.

1 The role of the medical profession in these responses needs to be explored, given that Stark, Flitcraft and Frazier (1979) have begun to study the processes by which they turn violence to women back upon the woman so that she becomes the problem. We need a British study of the processes they describe for similarities and differences. The British study would need to sample general practitioners as well as the casualty departments of hospitals, due to the fact that medical

services operate differently in the two countries, particularly for the poor.

2   Given the work of Stark, Flitcraft and Frazier and our own experience of the negative effects of drug taking, we need a British study of the prescription of tranquillizers and anti-depressants as a 'cure' for wife abuse. This is an aspect of focusing on the woman as the problem and, given the widespread prescription of these drugs, an investigation would seem to be a matter of urgency.

3   We also need a study of the efficacy of the treatment given to abused women admitted to mental hospitals, because electro convulsive therapy, or ECT is more frequently given to women than men, and for different reasons. We need to investigate the rationale for its use on abused women as this, too, is an aspect of turning the problem back upon the woman. While psycho-surgery is less frequent, its results can be even more extreme, and this should also be studied in relation to the abuse of women in the home.

4   We need a study of suicide and attempted suicide that seeks to elucidate the interconnection between violence in the home to women and their subsequent suicidal response.

Continued harassment and murder

Violence to women in the home is probably the most common form of violent crime. Estimates based on the analysis of police charge sheets by R. E. and R. Dobash reduce it to second place with wife abuse representing 25 per cent of all violent crimes. Until a national incidence study is completed we will not have accurate figures, but, even without these, it is clear that violence to women in the home is the largest single unchecked criminal activity going on in Britain today.

1   We need a study of women abused by their husbands or other men known to them who subsequently were murdered by these men in order to determine points at which there might have been effective intervention that could have saved these women. These cases should not be seen as aberrations but as one end of a continuum that begins with persistent harassment, moves through more verbal, sexual and extreme physical abuse, and ultimately ends in death.

2   We also need a study of women who continue to be abused by men even though they are divorced, have had injunctions, or have made strenuous efforts to leave the men behind by moving away, changing their names, etc. The process by which women are denied legal

protection or only partially given it needs systematic study through interviewing women.

3   While most women, in our experience, respond to violence against them in the home by internalizing the problem, on occasion women respond aggressively. We need studies of violence by women to men in all the criminal categories. We need to know how the criminal justice system processes women aggressors, how it differentiates between male and female cross-sex aggression, for example, in sentencing. We need to know more about the stress these women are under, how they come to adopt this solution and why other avenues of escape are not open to them. Carol Smart has begun work in this area, but a great deal more needs to be done (Smart 1976).

Immigration and nationality
Recent cases of Asian women who face deportation after having been abused and then abandoned or divorced raise the issue of the impact of immigration and nationality legislation on battered women. The general racism in British society further closes off options to women from other cultures and religious communities.

1   We need to document the effect of immigration and nationality legislation on battered women who are not British nationals who leave or are abandoned by their husbands or fiancés. We regard this as a priority area for research.

2   In our experience, women from other cultures and religious communities sometimes are unable to use services theoretically available to all because of fear of racism or anti-semitism. We need to explore how racism in British society further enslaves women and how it can be overcome.

Victim blaming
Women frequently blame themselves for assaults upon them, as does the wider society. This is very injurious to the individual concerned and an aspect of the work of WAFE is to help women overcome this destruction of the integrity of the self. Further, victim blaming adversely affects professional practice as the client is seen as unworthy of help and perhaps even as deserving of the assault. Victims of sexual abuse are so vulnerable to this response that rape, incest and other forms of sexual abuse of girls and women is only now surfacing as a problem of equal prominence to that of physical battering.

1   We need to examine how women's acceptance of responsibility for the violence men do to them creates the psychological vulnerability that ensures its continuation.

2   We need to examine the ways in which victim blaming is sex specific and how it is linked to sexual abuse and social subordination, as well as to pornography and the objectification of women.

3   We need to examine why professionals whose work is to help victims of male violence, blame the victims, and how they can be trained and supported to overcome this practice.

Abstract rights and actual remedies

A major emphasis of research in the areas of the criminal justice system, housing and income maintenance must be on finding ways to narrow the gap between the abstract rights of individual women and the actual remedies available to them. On the basis of our experience we suggest four areas in which the systematic collection of information would be helpful in doing this:

1   To delineate the gap between abstract rights and actual remedies available to women in the above areas.

2   To explore how the legislation frequently used by women who are abused by men is translated into social policy, and is administered; the impact and workings of different Acts of Parliament singly and on each other.

3   To locate the means by which the criminal justice system and local authorities frustrate the spirit, and even the letter, of national legislation and policy.

4   To establish the effects of current financial policies on the ability of women to achieve their abstract rights. If these are having an adverse effect, what can be done to reverse the trend?

We suggest the following specific studies:

1   The results of criminalizing violence to women in the home on the criminal justice system must be specified. We need a study which would estimate the increase in prisons, police, courts and their officials, including the probation service, that would be required in order to process all known offenders. This should be seen as a feasibility study.

2 We need to explore how violence to women in the house is reconstituted by the police and other officials in the criminal justice system as non-criminal. The concept and exercise of police discretion is one aspect to be studied, as are the various rationalizations offered for non-intervention such as victim blaming; for example, women do not pursue charges; women are said to have other remedies, particularly civil actions; other agencies can do it, especially social services; and re-labelling so that the fact that a man is attacking a woman is obscured, for example, the use of terms such as family dispute, domestic problem. Another aspect to be explored is the factors that are necessary for arrest to take place, for example, the man becomes abusive or violent to the police or to others who are involved, such as neighbours.

3 We need to examine the training methods and manuals for police and court officials in order to develop curriculum materials and techniques that will assist these men to assess crimes against the person as criminal activities when women are the victims. Pilot projects should be mounted with ongoing assessment an integral feature.

4 Women may be unwilling to use the legal processes that are available for the criminal prosecution of the men who abuse them. We need to study why this is so in order to find ways of increasing the numbers doing so. This would involve an examination of existing procedures, such as practices relating to bail and detaining men before they appear in court, and also the way in which women perceive and utilize criminal processes.

5 In our experience men attempt to use children in many ways to gain knowledge of the whereabouts of women so that they may continue their harassment, including initiating actions for custody or access. The granting of access and the lack of supervised access frequently causes extreme mental anguish and can put women and children in dangerous situations. We propose three areas for study:

    a court practice, including the effect of sexuality on decisions to determine patterns of response;

    b those situations where access arrangements are used to further harass women and children;

    c the preparation and recommendations of social inquiry reports need to be examined for an uncritical acceptance of the genuineness of the concern of the man for the children and the depth of concern for the safety of the woman.

6 We need further work to clarify how the state intervenes in

marriage through law and social policy. This would involve work on how the legal rules that define this relationship, its conduct and its termination reinforce female dependence on men; how the fiction of the unity of man and his wife through, for example, the operation of the supplementary benefit system, national insurance, income tax, legal decisions on custody, care and control and access to children, also serve to reinforce the dependence of women on men; and how the matter of mutual rights and duties has the same effect, because it is largely fiction. For example, the obligation to maintain, the principle duty of the male, should be studied for its effectiveness, alongside the social sanctions available to ensure that the wife services the male and the children.

7   As we have said in earlier submissions, the poorest women and children in the country live on housekeeping allowances not on supplementary benefit. We need a national survey to determine the extent of hidden poverty among women and children. Related to this is the need for studies of the effects of the recession on female employment and wages.

8   Legislation and recommendations for legislation in need of constant monitoring are:

  a   the Select Committee on Violence in Marriage;
  b   matrimonial law, particularly protection orders and injunctions, maintenance and its collection; guardianship, custody and access to children;
  c   income maintenance, particularly the Finer Committee recommendations and the Social Security Act 1980;
  d   housing and homelessness, particularly the Acts of 1976, 1977, and 1980.

9   Given the rapid changes in housing policies and housing availability, we need annual reviews of the housing needs of battered women.

10   Battered women are treated as if their problem is simply one of homelessness, but this is not the case. In our experience, upon re-housing a woman may be found by a persistent man, or access arrangements determined by the court will enable a man to find her. A woman may then take the man back, moving him into her new home, only to, yet again, find herself homeless as a result of further violence. It may be necessary for the woman to be rehoused again, possibly in another area. We need studies of how housing standards, location and administration limit or extend the possibilities of women achieving and maintaining an

independent life. We also need to consider the administrative means, for example national and local housing registers, whereby women can more easily change their area of residence. Greater flexibility is needed to eliminate housing as a system of social control of women for the benefit of men.

11 Local authorities vary in their regulations regarding the stage of proceedings for custody before rehousing. In our experience, some local authorities will rehouse a woman and her children with interim custody orders while others demand the permanent custody arrangements obtained on divorce. We need a national study of local authority practice because women and their children can experience great hardship if required to wait many months for rehousing. We also need to scrutinize the various forms these requirments may take for their legality.

12 The work of Mary Maynard on the social work response to violence to women in the home shows that social workers are frequently unable to recognize violence in their cases and, where they do, are often unable to respond appropriately to aid the victim (Maynard forthcoming). This is more than a question of personal attitudes because social workers often do not know the relevant legislation and law that would afford protection to their clients. In our experience, these same observations can be made of other professional groups. We therefore make two proposals:

a We need to devise curriculum input on violence to women for training courses for social workers, health visitors, doctors and nurses which should be monitored for its impact on attitudes towards and professional competence in helping victims.

b We need a handbook that would itemize good practice, in the way that the current handbook on child abuse does, covering all aspects and types of violence to women and girls. This should be aimed at a wide range of professional groups working in the fields of health, education, law, housing, social security and the personal social services.

The history of violence to women

We are only now becoming aware of the longstanding, firmly entrenched nature of violence to women by men in our society (May 1978; Tomes 1978; Lambertz 1979). The latter half of the nineteenth century, for example, saw concerted efforts to improve the position of women in relation to male conjugal rights and general sexual access. The campaign to repeal the Contagious Diseases Acts, for example, was part of a larger struggle to eliminate the double standard and there were voluntary societies concerned with violence to women and children in the home.

As we cannot understand the present without considering the past, we regard further historical work on violence to women to be a necessity. In particular, we need to examine how the issue was understood in various historical periods, the means by which it was raised and campaigns waged, and the solutions ultimately adopted, so that we can evaluate more accurately the ways to eliminate violence to women in all its many forms.

Study of incidence

We regard a national random incidence study of violence to women to be a priority. Serious consideration of violence to women, of necessity, includes determining its incidence, which can only be obtained by interviewing women. This is particularly pressing as our experience with battered women is that only a fraction of criminal aggression to women is dealt with by the criminal justice system which remains the sole source of statistical information. Thus far, there has been no British funding for an incidence study of male violence to women in and out of the home. J. Hanmer and S. Saunders are undertaking a pilot study of violence to women in Leeds with US funding and their ongoing work is the only attempt to ascertain directly from women information about reported and unreported acts of physical and sexual abuse. The major British victim study by Sparks, Genn and Dodd did not explore these areas (author's note, see p. 102).

A national incidence study would provide basic statistical information on:

1   The types of crimes that are committed against women and girls (these should not be limited to existing criminal categories of violence but should include subjective understandings and definitions held by women).
2   The amount of crime in each category.

3   The proportion and type of incidents that are processed by the criminal justice system.

But a national incidence study would do far more than provide necessary statistics. At its most general, the effect of this study would be to examine heterosexuality as a system of social relations as it is currently structured and how this system serves to normalize, even encourage, violence to women and female children. By collecting basic information on criminal attacks, it will be possible to further our understanding of a variety of issues:

1   The impact of one type of violence upon another; in particular the relationship between violence to women in the home and in public places. Violence to women in the home may be related to their restricted access to public space. We need to explore the connections between the use of public space by women and men, the reliance of women on male protection and attacks upon women. The vulnerability of woman to violent attacks in the home may be intensified by their reliance on men known to them in order to gain protection from men unknown to them. The majority of assailants of women are known to the women, wherever the assault takes place. The significance of this has yet to be explored.
2   The factors that create the conditions for the social definition of assault as non-assault:

  a   We need to look at how the social and legal acceptance of male conjugal rights contributes to physical and sexual abuse of women and female children. Rape is a crime so long as the parties are not married. We need to explore the ways in which the legality of rape in marriage affects the outcome of criminally defined rape. For example, rape, in relation to physical abuse, may be relatively under-reported and less frequently processed by the criminal justice system.
  b   We need to explore the importance of whether or not the assailant is known to the woman. A national incidence study will enable a variety of crimes to be examined for the influence of this factor which may be expressed in variety of ways:

    i   The definition of the attack as criminal or not by the criminal justice system and other parts of the state that may be involved, for example, social workers, medical services.

ii   Decisions about whether or not to proceed by the criminal justice system.

iii   Differential sentencing where the assault is processed by the criminal justice system.

iv   How the understanding of the attack by the woman victim is affected by her knowledge of the assailant.

3   How women respond when either assaults are defined as non-assaults by the criminal justice (and any other relevant state system), or when protection of the victim is ineffective. What measures do women take to protect themselves and their children from physical and sexual abuse when they are unable to secure their own protection? This is more than an individual response to an individual situation; for example, during the five years when the 'Ripper' roamed the North, many women fearing for their children's safety, as well as their own, seriously restricted their movements outside the home.

4   Life experiences that create greater vulnerability to male violence. A serious consideration of life experiences would enable us to overcome the mechanistic implications inherent in the use of socialization theory to explain why some women experience violence from men. For example, a national incidence study should give us more information on the known relationship between father–daughter incest and prostitution, where women are often subject to continuing sexual and physical abuse by men who use them either as customers or pimps.

5   The relationship between the cultural representations of women as acceptable victims of male sexual and physical assault and the actual behaviour of men. The recent extensions of the pornographic industry through shops and films, including home video, has created a qualitative as well as quantitative difference in the promotion of this ideology. Pornography can be widely defined as ranging from suggestive advertisements to hard core magazines; its aim is to portray women as sexually subordinate objects. The roles and scenes played out in pornography range from child molestations to violent torture, even murder. Linda Lovelace, for example, in her autobiography *Ordeal*, narrowly escaped with her life unlike Pat Malone who recently died acting out a bondage/suffocation fantasy for a policeman. A national incidence study will provide valuable information basic to a reconsideration of the importance of cultural representations in the creation and maintenance of the ideology that women are objects to be used.

If both men and women are interviewed it will be possible to explore the ways in which male violence to women differs from male violence to other men. It will be possible to examine for similarities and differences both the explanations for and the ways in which men commit violent crimes against women and children as opposed to men committing crimes against other men.

Linking the abuse of women and children in the home

The interconnections between violence to one or more family members needs serious consideration as neither child nor wife abuse can be properly understood if treated as unrelated. At present the real connection that may exist between the man abusing both his wife and child(ren) is ignored. In the literature child abuse is represented as if only mothers abuse their children in a family otherwise non-violent. This is far from the truth. While no accurate national statistics exist, it is estimated that in half of the child abuse cases the father is the aggressor. In our experience, men often abuse one or more of the children as well as the women with whom they live. This abuse may be sexual as well as physical and mental.

1   We need accurate information on the amount of sexual and physical abuse of children by social and biological fathers.
2   We need accurate statistics on how many and which family members men abuse and the type of abuse.
3   We need studies of incest and other forms of child sexual assault. Most family sexual abuse of children is fathers assaulting daughters. Our experience indicates that these crimes are far more widespread than that conveyed by criminal statistics and they are often linked with wife abuse. These studies should investigate the options open to women to protect their children when they are unable to protect themselves.

This information could be collected as part of a national incidence study, but there is also a place for smaller non-random studies.

Conclusion

This paper has been prepared by the research group of WAFE on the instructions of member groups. It has been circulated for comment and approval and represents our collective view on the way forward for research on violence to women in the home.

Research group, WAFE
September 1981

Current research studies

Studies sponsored by the Home Office

Centre for Criminological Research
12 Bevington Road
Oxford
Oxford 53171

Joanna Shapland is carrying out a follow-up study of those victims in the sample (from the Victim in the Criminal Justice System project) who applied for compensation from the Criminal Injuries Compensation Board. This was published in 1982.

Centre for Socio-Legal Studies
Wolfson College
Oxford
Oxford 52967

The 'Misfortune Project' has examined existing networks of compensatory and supportive systems available to the injured, disabled and seriously ill. A book on compensation was published in 1982 (Home Office Research & Planning Unit) including a chapter on the Criminal Injuries Compensation Scheme.

Home Office Research & Planning Unit
50 Queen Anne's Gate
London SW1
231 3000

Community services for victims of crime
The aim of the project is to ascertain to which agencies in the community victims of crime turn for help and advice, what services those

agencies provide, and how far they meet the needs of victims. The project was planned in two parts.

The first part had two main objectives: to assess the nature and extent of victim support schemes and the services they provide (by means of a questionnaire sent by NAVSS to affiliated schemes); and to survey other agencies aiding victims, to assess numbers of victims dealt with, types of crime involved, services provided, and sources of referral. The research report was available in 1983 (Karen Williams, *Community Resources for Victims of Crime*).

The second part of the study aims to survey victims' views and use of services provided by victim support schemes and other agencies.

National Crime Survey

A random sample of 10,905 people were interviewed throughout England and Wales at the beginning of 1982. (The Scottish Office has conducted a parallel survey with a sample of around 5000). The aim of the survey was to acquire further knowledge on the extent of crime, and thus help in the interpretation of official statistics. One aim was to find out how much crime goes unreported and why people choose not to report crimes to the police. It is hoped that the survey will be repeated every three years and will thus provide information about crime trends independent of official statistics.

The survey aims to provide new information about the impact of crime on victims – the financial impact, the extent of any physical injuries, and the emotional consequences in terms of the fear of crime. Initial findings were available in spring 1983 (*The British Crime Survey 1983*).

Note: It is likely that a great deal of importance will be attached to the British Crime Survey and the results will be used to undermine concern about violence to women.

The first report was published during the preparation of this book. We quote in full their comments on offences against women to show the inadequacy of their research:

Offences against women
Something should be said about offences against women – 'wife battering', indecent assault, attempted rape and rape. A small minority (10%) of assault victims were women who had been assaulted by their present or previous husbands or boyfriends. This proportion may well be an underestimate. Many

such victims may be unprepared to report incidents of this nature to an interviewer; they may not feel that assaults of this sort fall within the survey's scope, or they may feel embarrassment or shame. Indeed, their assailant may be in the same room at the time of interview.

The survey showed a very low rate for rape and other sexual offences. In fact, only one rape was uncovered, and that was an attempt. This reflected the rarity of sexual attacks by complete strangers. However, leaving aside definitional problems and any sampling error, some undercounting of such offences committed by non-strangers may have arisen from respondents' reluctance to relive a painful or embarrassing experience for the benefit of a survey interviewer. (*The British Crime Survey*, p. 21)

We can see from the experiences and results of the Leeds study that criticisms made by Home Office researchers are valid. The cost of a national 11,000 household survey must run into several hundred thousand pounds and this is all that they have to say about women. These results prove, once again, that the only reliable research about women must come from women.

The Police Foundation
18–20 Elvian House
St Andrew's Street
London EC4
01–583 3432

The Metropolitan police force is running a neighbourhood policing project in several areas. The Police Foundation is evaluating the project over a two year period. Victims support schemes may be set up, or strengthened where already in existence in the experimental areas during the project.

Scottish Home and Health Department
St Andrew's House
Edinburgh
031–556 8501

There is a high drop-out rate throughout the Scottish criminal justice system of prosecutions for sexual assault. This study aims to follow cases through the system, partly to gain a clearer idea of factors which influence the decision to prosecute. The research is largely based on interviews with women who have reported sexual assaults, and with the police, and on official records.

Victim–police interaction and its effects on public attitudes to the police
John Howley – MSc – Cranfield Institute of Technology

The manner in which police deal with victims of crime is largely based upon a number of assumptions about what the public expects police to do when crimes are reported. This research sought to test the validity of some of those assumptions by interviewing victims of residential burglary, and by discussion with police officers, individually and in groups.

Alan Phipps – PhD – Middlesex Polytechnic

An examination of the emergence of concern with criminal victimization in the United States and Britain in the 1960s and 1970s, and the part this concern has played in policy formation and in theory and practice within criminology.

Reparation and mediation in criminal justice
Martin Wright – PhD – London School of Economics and Political
    Science

The project will examine the proportion, outlined in the book *Making Good* (Wright 1982), that some of the difficulties inherent in a criminal justice system based on penal and rehabilitative models could be avoided in a model based on reparation. In this context the development of mediation and restitution schemes in the USA and Australia, and other cross-cultural parallels, will be examined. Since the model places less emphasis on deterrence, and indeed stresses its disadvantages, the potential of other approaches to crime reduction will be explored. Possible difficulties will also be considered, such as absolute liability, attempts, etc., and there will be an assessment of the extent to which the model could meet the main prerequisites of the criminal justice process such as fairness, satisfaction among participants and the public, and reduction in the use of imprisonment.

Other surveys

We can lend women copies of the following questionnaires and project reports. We think you will find these of particular interest.

1 National crime survey referred to earlier.
2 Diana Russell interviewed just under 1000 women in San Francisco on their experiences of sexual violence. One question dealt with rape in marriage and the results are published (*Rape in Marriage* 1982). The remainder of the information has yet to be written up.
3 Mark A. Schulman interviewed 1793 married or cohabiting women for the Kentucky Commission on Women, a state government agency. He approached the question of violence indirectly and, judging from the results, successfully. The questionnaire began with, 'The purpose of this study is to learn about the way family disagreements are settled.' After exploring non-violent and verbal ways, questions were asked about direct violence. The survey was by telephone, a possible approach as almost every home in the US has one (*A Survey of Spousal Violence Against Women In Kentucky* 1979).
4 *The Park Slope Safe Homes Project Manual* from Brooklyn, New York, gives details about setting up a community based programme for battered women and their families. We have many criticisms and reservations about this project, but the manual provides useful ideas which could be adapted for a 'safe house' project, such as the Cambridge, Massachusetts, project.

You may wish to contact the following researchers for copies of their questionnaires.

1 Jan Pahl, University of Kent, Canterbury. She studied the Women's Aid refuge at Canterbury and later questioned women who had left the refuge.
2 Liz Kelly, Department of Sociology, University of Essex. Liz is interviewing women about experiences of incest, rape and domestic violence.
3 Sue Gorbing, Department of Law, University of Birmingham. Sue is looking at the effectiveness of injunctions for battered women.
4 Betsy Stanko, Clark University, 950 Main Street, Worcester, Massachusetts 01610. Betsy was in Britain in 1983 looking at how the police decide to go ahead with prosecutions of violence to women.

5   Marguerite Russell, School of Applied Social Studies, University of Bradford, West Yorkshire. Marguerite is looking at the murder of women.

6   Rebecca Emerson Dobash and Russell Dobash, Department of Sociology, Stirling University, Scotland. Rebecca and Russell have been working on violence to women in the home for the past decade. They have analysed police actions as well.

7   Cleveland Refuge and Aid for Women and Children, Middlesborough, Tyne and Wear. Funded by the Equal Opportunities Commission to study the problems faced by women seeking to escape domestic violence in circumstances of unequal access to economic and social resources.

8   London Rape Crisis, PO Box 69, London, WC1X 9NJ. Funded by the Equal Opportunities Commission to analyse the data collected by this group since 1976 in order to increase the availability of factual information on rape and sexual assault and to assess the impact that fear of such assault has on women's access to equality of opportunity.

9   Leeds Trade Union and Community Resource and Information Centre (TUCRIC), Market Buildings, Vicar Lane, Leeds 1. Funded by the Equal Opportunities Commission to investigate the nature and extent of sexual harassment at work in a variety of workplaces, to suggest guidelines for employers and employees and to make recommendations for any appropriate changes in legislation.

Projects 7, 8 and 9 are the sole contribution of the Equal Opportunities Commission to research on violence to women. This agency is funded by the Home Office which keeps a sharp eye on the interpretation of the criteria to be used by the Commissioners in deciding on grant applications. For example, we submitted a project in October 1981 to continue our research to be told to re-submit it if we took out the section on the police.

10   Sandra McNeill, c/o WAVAW, Market Buildings, Vicar Lane, Leeds 1. Sandra has completed a study of indecent exposure in which she interviewed women about their experiences of flashing.

11   Jill Radford, Wandsworth Policing Campaign, 248–50 Lavender Hill, London SW11. This GLC funded project is interviewing women about their experiences of violence and the police response.

Appendix

Peter Sutcliffe (widely referred to as the 'Ripper' or even 'Jack' (the Ripper)) was charged with the murder of thirteen women and the attempted murder of seven others at Dewsbury Magistrates Court on 20 February 1981.

He was charged with the murder of:

Wilma McCann, aged 28, of Scott Hall Avenue, Chapeltown, Leeds, in Leeds on 30 October 1975. She had four children.

Emily Monica Jackson, aged 42, of Back Green, Churwell, Morley, Leeds, in Leeds on or about 20 January 1976. She had three children.

Irene Richardson, aged 28, of Cowper Street, Chapeltown, Leeds, in Leeds on or about 6 February 1977. She had two children.

Patricia Atkinson, aged 33, of Oak Avenue, Manningham, Bradford, in Bradford on 23 April 1977. She had three children.

Jayne Michelle MacDonald, aged 16, of Scott Hall Road, Leeds, in Leeds on 26 June 1977.

Jean Bernadette Jordan, aged 21, of Lingbeck Crescent, Hulme, Manchester, in Manchester between 30 September and 11 October 1977. She had two children.

Yvonne Ann Pearson, aged 22, of Woodbury Street, Bradford, in Bradford between 20 January and 26 March 1978. She had two children.

Helen Maria Rytka, aged 18, of Elmfield Avenue, Birkby, Huddersfield, in Huddersfield between 30 January and 4 February 1978.

Vera Evelyn Millward, aged 40, of Grenham Avenue, Hulme, Manchester, in Manchester on or about 16 May 1978. She had seven children.

Josephine Anne Whittaker, aged 19, of Ivy Street, Halifax, in Halifax on or about 4 April 1979.

Barbara Janine Leach, aged 20, of Grove Terrace, Bradford, in Bradford between 1 and 4 September 1979.
Marguerite Walls, aged 47, of New Park Croft, Farsley, Leeds, in Farsley on or about 20 August 1980.
Jacqueline Hill, aged 20, of Lupton Flats, Headingley, Leeds, in Headingley between 16 and 19 November 1980.

Attempted murder of:

Anna Patricia Rogulski, aged 39, at Keighley on 5 July 1975.
Olive Smelt, aged 51, at Halifax on or about 15 August 1975.
Marcella Claxton, aged 25, at Leeds on 9 May 1976.
Maureen Long, aged 46, at Leeds on 10 July 1977.
Marylin Moore, aged 28, at Leeds on 14 December 1977.
Dr Upadhya Nadavathy Bandara, aged 34, at Leeds on 24 September 1980.
Teresa Simone Sykes, aged 16, at Huddersfield on 5 November 1980.

Sutcliffe was given a life sentence for murder on 22 May 1981. Mr Justice Boreham, sentencing Sutcliffe, said he hoped life imprisonment 'would mean precisely that', but because he could not, in law, order that Sutcliffe spend the rest of his life in jail, the judge said he would recommend to the Home Secretary that Sutcliffe remain in prison for a minimum of thirty years. Meanwhile, the struggle still goes on to define Sutcliffe as 'mad'. Dr Hugo Milne, a forensic psychiatrist from Bradford is undeterred in his fight to get Sutcliffe transferred from prison to a special hospital. The Home Secretary has so far refused, but as *The Guardian* reports (11 October 1982) 'Sutcliffe's treatment has provoked a bitter dispute between the Home Office and psychiatrists, who have privately warned Whitehall officials that the case has opened a dangerous breach between medicine and law.' Transfer to mental hospital would not only obscure the meaning of these crimes against women, but would also enable Sutcliffe to obtain legal aid for repeated appeals against his hospital confinement.

Suggested further reading

Binney, Val, Harkell, Gina, and Nixon, Judy (1981), *Leaving Violent Men*, Women's Aid Federation England

Borkowski, Margaret, Murch, Mervyn, and Walker, Valerie (1983), *Community Reponse to Marital Violence*. Final report to DHSS, London: Tavistock

Catlin, Gary, and Murray, Susan (1979), *Report on Canadian Victimisation Survey Methodological Pretests*, Ottowa: Statistics Canada

Criminal Statistics England and Wales (published annually), HMSO

Dobash, Rebecca Emerson, and Dobash, Russell (1980), *Violence Against Wives: A Case Against the Patriarchy*, London: Open Books

Evason, Eileen (1982), *Hidden Violence: A Study of Battered Women in Northern Ireland*, Belfast: Farset Co-operative Press

Gamarnikow, Eva, Morgan, David, Purvis, June, and Taylorson, Daphne (1983), *The Public and the Private*, London: Heinemann

Hanmer, Jalna (1978), 'Male violence and the social control of women', in Gary Littlejohn, Barry Smart, John Wakeford, and Nira Yuval-Davies (eds.), *Power and the State*, London: Croom Helm

Hanmer, Jalna, and Leonard, Diana (forthcoming), 'Negotiating the problem: the DHSS and research on violence in marriage', in Colin Bell, and Helen Roberts (eds.), *Social Researching: Problems, Politics and Practice*, London: Routledge and Kegan Paul

Hough, Mike, and Mayhew, Pat (1983), *The British Crime Survey: First Report*. A Home Office Research and Planning Unit Report, Home Office Research Study no. 76, London: HMSO

London Rape Crisis Centre, First Report (1977), *Second Report* (1978), *Third Report* (1982), Rape Crisis Centre, PO Box 42, London N6 5BU

McNeill, Sandra (1982), 'Flashing: its effect on women', MA thesis, University of York (A copy is also held by the Women's Research and Resources Centre, Hungerford House, Victoria Embankment, London WC2.)

Malamuth, Neil M., and Check, James V. P., (1981), 'The effects of mass media exposure on acceptance of violence against women: a field experiment', *Journal of Research in Personality*, **15**, pp. 436–46

Maynard, Mary (forthcoming), 'The response of social workers to domestic violence', in Jan Pahl (ed.), *Private Violence and Public Policy*, London: Routledge and Kegan Paul

Oakley, Ann (1981), 'Interviewing women: a contradiction in terms', in Helen Roberts (ed.), *Doing Feminist Research*, London: Routledge and Kegan Paul

Pahl, Jan (1978), *A Refuge for Battered Women*, London: HMSO

Pahl, Jan (1981), *A Bridge Over Troubled Waters*, unpublished report to the DHSS

Pahl, Jan (1983), 'Violence unpublished', *New Society*, **64**, p. 105

Rafter, Nicole Hahn, and Stanko, Elizabeth Anne (eds.) (1982), *Judge, Lawyer, Victim, Thief: Women, Gender Role and Criminal Justice*, Chicago: Northeastern University Press

Russell, Diana E. H. (1982), *Rape in Marriage*, New York: Macmillan

Shapland, Joanna, Willmore, Jon, and Duff, Peter (1981), *The Victim and the Criminal Justice System*. Final report to the Home Office (to be published by Macmillan)

Skogan, Wesley G. (1981), *Issues in the Measurement of Victimisation*, Washington DC: Department of Justice, NCJ–74682

Sparks, Richard, Genn, Hazel, and Dodd, David (1977), *Surveying Victims*, New York: Wiley

Stark, Evan, Flitcraft, Anne, and Frazier, W. (1979), 'Medicine and patriarchal violence: the social construction of a "private" event', *International Journal of Health Services*, **9** no. 3, pp. 461–92

Turner, Anthony G. (1972), *The San Jose Methods Test of Known Crime Victims*, Washington DC: National Criminal Justice Information and Statistics Service, Law Enforcement Assistance Administration, US Department of Justice

Postscript

While we were writing this book we were, co-incidently, being harassed by the West Yorkshire Police. Their first call was about arson attacks on sex/video shops in a suburb of Leeds and the second and third were about the attempted bombing of the Leeds Conservative Party head-quarters. The last visit involved a thorough search of our home. The papers taken were correspondence from well-known women academics and publishers in Britain regarding a French feminist theoretical journal, *Nouvelles Questions Feministes*, whose editor-in-chief is Simone de Beauvoir, one copy of a British feminist women-only magazine, and a graduate student's essay on menstruation.

We share our home with one other woman, our children and numer-ous pets. The only organizations we belong to are Women's Aid and the British Sociological Association. Our only 'crimes' are to help indi-vidual women who have been abused, and to write about violence from men to women, including how little the police do to protect women from attack by men in Britain generally and in West Yorkshire in particular.

The only women in all three interviews that we were asked if we knew was the chairperson of the licensing sub-committee of Leeds City Council. She was on record as opposing snuff movies in which women are physically and sexually abused and finally murdered and her com-mittee was at the time considering the licenses for sex shops in Leeds. Many women, including Labour Party constituency members, are incensed by the growth of the distribution of pornography in Leeds and want it stopped. But do the police? The experience of those of us who work in Women's Aid is that the police do little to protect women from actual violence, and our research offers further information on and insight into their lack of response. Why then should they be concerned about the representation of violence to women, an industry which generates millions of pounds of profit!

We conclude that to dare to speak out is to have a police file made on you; to be 'lifted' without evidence. But as feminist theory largely comes from experience, this is a two-way process. For our files this experience is yet another example of how male violence to women is socially sanctioned.

The public have few ways to question police behaviour. We have made an official complaint, but our experience of this type of action on behalf of battered women is that, as the investigation is entirely internal, nothing much happens. The public is not permitted to know what so-called evidence, if any, is asked for or offered to magistrates when the police request search warrants. If the 'evidence' seized from us had to be related to admissible evidence in court, we think it unlikely that the items above would have been taken (they have now all been returned). Further, we think that if the police had to provide reasonable grounds to obtain search warrants, they would not have come to our home.

The new Police and Criminal Evidence Bill will give police even more power than they have now. Already they harass members of the black and Irish communities in Britain. Now they are seriously moving in on women. Rather than giving the police more power we should be demanding less power and more accountability to women. When we demand curfew on men we mean policemen also. Our strength must be in our women's groups and organizations. We have to organize to protect ourselves and our children from all forms of male violence and control. If any women have recently faced similar forms of police harassment, please write and tell us about it. It is only by pooling all our experiences that we effectively challenge patriarchal power.